OWN IT!

The UPS and DOWNS of Homebuying for Women Who Go It Alone

Jennifer Musselman

SEAL PRESS

Own It!
The Ups and Downs of Homebuying for Women Who Go It Alone

Published by
Seal Press
A Member of Perseus Books Group
1700 Fourth Street
Berkeley, California

Library of Congress Cataloging-in-Publication Data

Musselman, Jennifer, 1973-
  Own it! : the ups and downs of homebuying for women who go it alone / by Jennifer Musselman.
    p. cm.
  ISBN-13: 978-1-58005-230-6
  ISBN-10: 1-58005-230-4
  1. House buying. 2. Single women. I. Title.

HD1390.5.M87 2008
643'.1208652--dc22

                          2007040913

Cover design by Gia Giasullo
Interior design by Megan Cooney
Printed in the United States of America
Distributed by Publishers Group West

To Leo, my reason to rush home.

Contents

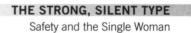

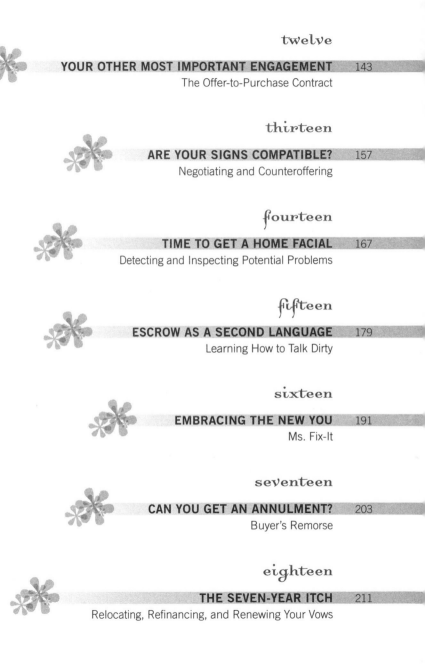

Introduction

What—or Who—Are You Waiting For?

Ever since I was a little girl, I've played house. It started with my kindergarten friends. We'd meticulously build our "home" during playdates, using the ends of coffee tables and couches as lumber, and blankets and pillows as roofing. Sometimes the "roof" caved in when a treacherous G.I. Joe hailstorm hit our make-believe town. But in those days, one loud cry to Mom or a good old-fashioned big-sister thumping repaired the roof instantaneously.

Eventually, I graduated to a more sophisticated version of playing house when, at age eighteen, I briefly moved in with my older, more "mature" boyfriend. Tommy was twenty-three and owned his own home in small-town Iowa. Oh, did I think we were well on our way to adulthood.

Tommy let me decorate the bedroom just the way my little heart desired. The rest of the house, well, that was his playroom.

1

Still, I proudly scrubbed the bathroom spotless from time to time, ferociously vacuumed the living room, and slaved in the kitchen, perfecting my new, delicious meal of Crock-Pot–cooked pork chops in mushroom soup.

In some regard, I kind of had it made back then. It was Tommy's place, so he incurred the mortgage and all utility bills. Meanwhile, I cleaned and cooked when I pleased. It was fun. After all, I was still *playing* house.

Oh, yes, all was peachy, except that when any major blowup happened, one of us would storm out. And since it was clearly Tommy's home, you guessed it—I was usually the one who was sent packing. I'd gather up all my valuables, which consisted mainly of a closet full of clothes and shoes, toiletries, and a pillow, and shove them into my rundown car in the middle of a freezing winter night. I always had the safe haven of my sister's house, which she shared with her husband and two sons. Their nicely finished basement supplied me with a warm shelter and a blow-up mattress when I needed to crash for a few nights—or indefinitely.

Those early years of playing house with a man were a telescope into a future I knew I did not want—a life peppered with unpredictability and insecurity. It revealed how I didn't want to depend on a man for my happiness and security. I wanted a partner—not a man to take care of me the way a father takes care of his child—and a home where my opinion and feelings could be heard without fear that my stability might crumble beneath me.

I yearned to feel safe and protected. I wanted to feel confident about my future. To attain this goal, I realized I would need to knit a safety net for myself. This way, my security couldn't be abruptly pulled out from underneath me. If I made it, stitch by stitch, it was mine to keep.

I trusted a small collection of loving and dependable friends and family members for emotional support when everyday life dealt me too many crappy cards. I didn't want to rely on any one person to provide my security in life. I wanted to be a woman who was happy, capable, and financially stable on her own. I could lean on friends, family, and mentors for help or advice. It felt important to me to have a safety net that would never fail me, and I knew that had to come from within.

And that's just what I set out to do in my twenties: build a good career, form strong friendships, and travel the world. But life began to shift as I broached my thirties. Financially, I was taking a tax hit from the government for making a modest but decent salary as a single woman.

Emotionally, I was feeling ready to share my life with someone and nurture my more domestic side. It was a side I'd neglected in favor of tackling corporate America and securing my financial future. Now my nesting instincts were resurfacing. I wanted to learn to cook and host grown-up dinner parties in a home I could be proud of. I also wanted a dog. Landlords and roommates compromised my options. And so, both financially and emotionally prepared, I decided I would buy a home—even if I had to go it alone.

I entered my new world with much trepidation. Information about loans, down payments, taxes, and contractual obligations was dizzying and confusing. But beneath my anxiety, the anticipation of really purchasing a property all on my own pulsated through my body. This was a chance to grow and prove to myself that I was capable of anything I set my mind to.

Six months later, while I was still looking for the right home, I met Ken. I thought I'd met my Mr. Right. He moved quickly to infiltrate my time and my life. But as ready as I was to make a life together, I couldn't just give up the life I'd built before, the life I'd delicately chiseled over thirty years. I was careful to balance my independence with my newfound coupledom, and to continue my pursuit of buying a home alone.

About three months into our relationship, I was sent into a whirlwind. Ken, as it turned out, revealed he was against the whole idea of my buying a home alone. I was both bewildered and jolted by his response. My independent spirit kicked me in the gut, pleading me to fight for its preservation.

The intense argument that ensued revealed the truth: Ken had just suppressed his hurt and disappointment that I was thinking of making such a commitment without him. He wondered how he fit into my life . . . or *if* he did.

I felt suffocated. I needed him to support my dream, not hold me back from it. It was a feat I needed to accomplish for my emotional well-being. I encouraged him to be a part of it, not financially, but by remodeling the home into a place we could both be proud of and perhaps eventually share. Instead, he saw the process as a monumental gesture that threatened our future, and believed that I didn't need him.

I didn't put an offer on any of those initial condos. None of them were quite the right fit. Turns out, neither was Ken. The upside was that all the second-guessing I grappled with about buying a home on my own instantly evaporated with the dissolution of my relationship. I was reminded of what my heart already knew: Sharing life adventures and responsibilities with a partner is a gift, but it doesn't ensure happiness or security. You do. So what—or who—are you waiting for?

one

THE EMOTIONAL ROLLER COASTER

The Highs and Lows of House Hunting as a Single Woman

With my life coming together, primarily in my career and ensuing financial stability, my lifelong dream was within reach. Instead of *playing* house, now I could realistically buy one—my own home. I longed to decorate, clean, cook, or leave the house a total mess. But most of all, I longed for the stability that only your own home can offer. So why, as my dream appeared more attainable, did it seem larger than life and even scarier?

Just like on the first day of kindergarten, I wanted someone to hold my hand, someone I could run to if the process of buying and owning my own home got to be too scary. I wanted to go through with it, but if it all got to be too much and I wanted out, I wanted to know that I could walk away at any point and be okay.

My fears about this process were so immobilizing that I realized I needed to examine them further. After all, wasn't I the

7

once-starry-eyed girl with an uncertain future who'd driven half-
way across the country at age eighteen, with very little money in
her pocket, in search of her dreams? Now I was standing on a cliff
overlooking the beautiful beach city of Santa Monica, California,
contemplating buying a home but afraid to take the leap. What
had happened to me?

I realized that even though I was older, wiser, and more self-
sufficient than ever, I was holding my homeowning dream cap-
tive, using a plethora of excuses to prevent its realization: "I don't
have enough for a 20 percent down payment"; "I still have a lot
of places I want to travel to"; "I'm waiting for the market to
turn to get more bang for my buck"; and (my personal favorite)
"What if I lose my job tomorrow?" (despite the fact that I'd been
employed by the same company for nearly a decade). Yet each
excuse sounded very rational, even responsible. But then, so do
the justifications I continue to console myself with when it comes
to losing the extra ten pounds I've been wanting to lose for the
past ten years.

Yep, if you look hard enough, a multitude of obstacles can
stand in the way of realizing your hopes and dreams. Staying safe
in wanting mode, after all, is a whole lot easier than being vulnerable to failure, no matter what your goal is.

After a bit of soul searching, I realized, sadly, that the only
thing truly holding me back was the one thing I'd sworn never
would: the support of a man. I was aghast and ashamed. Had
the Cinderella storytelling and my own mother's modeling during my childhood unknowingly seeped into my subconscious and
made me feel this way? Or was Mother Nature to blame? I wasn't

certain—but what I did know was that I wasn't alone in feeling this way.

Take my friend Tara, for instance. Tara is a sharp, thirty-four-year-old attorney for the City of Los Angeles with a girl-next-door approachability and fun-loving attitude. She is pretty, pulled together, and shifting to the next stage of her life: creating a family of her own.

For nearly a decade, Tara dated Sam, a man she met at a part-time retail job while putting herself through law school. Tara eventually left that gig to accomplish her career goals, while Sam stayed on full-time as a salesman. Tara tried for years to overlook his nonchalant approach to his future, their future, because she loved him and they got along well. But Sam's lackadaisical approach to his career ambitions spilled into his attitude toward marriage, kids, and homeowning. He talked about "someday" with Tara, but never planned for it.

In keeping with a female-fantasy cliché, Tara had always dreamed of standing before her white picket fence hand in hand with her Prince Charming—blissfully secure about undertaking their shared adventure. She never truly considered buying a home on her own, despite the fact that she was financially able to. And why not? Was it because she'd be admitting defeat, be forced to sacrifice the dream—the whole happily ever after picture—that she'd held on to since she was a little girl? The answer is yes—for Tara and many other women—even though admitting this idea would make many modern women cringe.

My friend Maria, an ambitious, thirty-three-year-old advertising executive, also fell victim to this plight. In 2002, she and her boyfriend, Matt, decided to buy a home in the posh neighborhood of Bel-Air, California. "Buying a home with Matt was exciting," Maria says. "It was symbolic of our intentions to be married one day, and was just a wise investment for our future."

Two years into living together, Matt and Maria agreed to go their separate ways. Family support and her personal savings enabled Maria to qualify for a second loan to buy Matt out of his share of the home, and they were able to split cleanly and amicably. "Living together made us realize we weren't right for each other after all. Our breakup was painful. But in reflection, I can honestly say that had Matt and I not initially bought the house together, I don't know that I'd have considered doing it by myself," Maria admits. "Of course, I was petrified to take on the mortgage alone once we decided to break up. But now I chuckle that I was ever afraid."

I knew how Tara and Maria felt. Knowing someone's in it with you makes most challenges of this magnitude more comfortable. Astonishingly, even once I'd decided to go it alone and begun gathering experts and family and friends for support, I sometimes silently questioned if I was going to be okay once I finally went through with it. You see, the arduous process of picking the right realtor and learning about mortgages, taxes, and my credit only stirred the whisper of doubt within me. But I tried to not look back and instead trusted in my decision . . . and in myself. Two and a half years later, I finally found the right condo, nestled in the industrial part of sunny Santa Monica.

My friends and family and I celebrated my feat. We cheered my capability—alone, I had achieved a piece of the American dream! Nothing and nobody can take that kind of inner strength away from you once you take the plunge, although certain people will try to in one way or another. But you will surmount these obstacles and emerge a stronger, wiser woman—just as I have.

THE 411

Real estate is an ever-changing industry. Trendy neighborhoods, housing markets, and interest rates fluctuate regularly. Once you've read up on the basics of homebuying in this book and have gathered your team of people to help you—like a realtor, inspector, insurance representative, and mortgage lender—don't stop doing your homeowning homework. Throughout the house-hunting process, keep up with events in the newspaper or online that might affect the housing market in the region in which you intend to buy. You will also want to consistently monitor interest rates and loan options available to you. Depending on how long your hunt takes, these variables will likely change. Even the slightest change in the real estate climate can adversely affect if and where you buy, how much you spend, and whether a mortgage lender loans you the funds you may need.

When I was going through the honeymoon phase with my new house, my strength was tested definitively. Within the first few months, my worries about leaky faucets, property taxes, and home and earthquake insurance sprouted, seeded by my lack of experience and by flying solo in this adventure. Yes, the fear lingered, but it also subsided with each passing month that I successfully caught the curveballs thrown my way. And after taking each issue in stride, I settled comfortably into my new home, my new life, with pride.

I love my humble little abode. It's not that it's lavish or even spacious—I love it because it's mine. With ownership comes freedom. Ironically, I feared that tying myself to a mortgage would mean sacrificing my freedom. In reality, owning has empowered me with more security, choices, and rights to live as I please. Unlike in renting, as a homeowner, you hold your destiny in your hands. You determine your monthly housing expenses. You decide if you sell or remodel. Most important, it is undeniably satisfying to know that your monthly payments are investing in your future, not someone else's.

Surprisingly, and much to my chagrin, one unforeseen challenge has surfaced since I bought my white picket fence all by my lonesome: Qualified dates have become sparse. I used to think my pool of dating candidates had actually decreased. It seemed as if I would become less appealing to some men once they learned I was a homeowner. Dumbfounded? I was too, so I couldn't help but wonder: *Can a woman be too pulled together?*

I informally polled my personal male army, consisting of a few of my professional, early- to late-thirties good guy friends and my twenty-seven-year-old little brother, on just that. They all agreed, uniformly, that if a woman is nicely dressed, has a good job, and owns her own home, it wouldn't deter them from being attracted to her. After all, they exclaimed, hot is hot! But would they pursue a relationship with a woman who appeared to "have it all"?

"It *is* intimidating," said my friend Taylor. "You wonder how you measure up if you're not in the same place. How is she going to need you?" Most of the men admitted that somewhere in their subconscious minds, their need to be "heroes" to the women they dated was ingrained. Hence the dilemma: How do the men still seeking princesses to save fare with many of today's strong, financially independent single women?

Fortunately, other men I polled—some with careers in sales, investment banking, and law, others bartenders and teachers—disagreed. "A woman who is attractive, smart, and accomplished is sexy," they said, adding, "She still needs you. You just have to figure out how."

Then, after a date with an aspiring actor/bartender who appeared to be in awe of my accomplishments, an important realization dawned on me: Dating had become more difficult not so much because men found me less attractive since I'd bought my home, but more because I'd grown less interested in dating someone who wasn't accomplished in his own life. Buying my own home had the effect of quickly weeding out men who weren't secure with themselves. The truth is, women shouldn't be worried if a man is scared away because we own our own homes. That's a blessing in disguise, after all. The question strong, smart, and accomplished women should be asking themselves is: *Can this person give me what I need? And if not, why am I willing to settle for anything less?*

Many modern women choose not to heed a relationship structure that they believe is archaic, in which they rely on a man to bring home the bacon and provide a nice, safe home for his wife and children. We have more options today, and our needs, particularly where a partner is concerned, aren't so one-dimensional—or solely financially based. Plenty of women have no intention of marrying or ever having children, and live in nontraditional relationships that may or may not ever include living with their partners.

Albeit not without some scrutiny, much of society today is far more accepting of a woman's right to choose a nontraditional lifestyle. Additionally, as women have made more and more strides in the professional, financial, and social arenas, their empowerment has led to more egalitarian relationships between dating partners. As a result, couples have fewer defined "rules" and more room to define their individual roles within their relationships.

As for me, while I feel blessed to be self-sufficient enough to afford my own home, I would still welcome the support and companionship of a partner in my life. Between taking charge in the office, acting as president of my homeowners' association, and now being a mom to my adorable and playful new puppy, Leo, I feel ready to invite a partner to take on some of my responsibilities at home. Having a dependable partner—whether he took Leo for long walks, consoled me when I was exhausted from my workday, unloaded groceries, planned trips, or shared in my mortgage expense—would surely make my fast-paced life more relaxing. But not even meeting my Prince Charming could supersede the incredible feelings of reward and accomplishment I've had since buying my home. And the fact that I did it alone only makes me appreciate this gift more.

Remember my friend Tara? She eventually left her uncertain future with her ten-year boyfriend, Sam, and is now happily dating Tom, a man who is also a city attorney and owns his own home. He has been encouraging Tara to stop putting off her house hunt. He admires her for her accomplishments and wants her to be financially savvy for herself. While he wants to be able to "take care" of her, he is confident that he can and does, in a way that doesn't preclude her striving for her own self-sufficiency and independence. Their relationship is strong because they both want the same thing for each other: to be the most fulfilled individuals they can be.

two

GROWING OUT YOUR ROOTS

Are You Ready for a Change?

In my prepubescent years, I daydreamed often about my future. I was certain I had a journey to uncover beyond my one-highway hometown. Unlike some kids today, who seem to have the whole world at their fingertips, most kids in my town in the eighties grew up with good ol' television. TV served as my portal to what lived and breathed outside of my Midwestern middle-school universe of boy-next-door crushes, JCPenney fashion, and church social gatherings.

One afternoon after school, I flipped through the channels, trying to select from a plethora of pixellated programs. The one that caught my eye featured a tall, lean brunette cloaked in the most beautiful clothes my small-town Iowan eyes had ever seen. I was enraptured by her beauty, and by the way she came alive amid her surroundings: skyscrapers, bustling taxis and buses, and briefcase-carrying men and women, all abuzz. As the sun

onscreen peeked through the gigantic buildings and lit up her
face, I felt an unfamiliar, pulsating energy. I had just witnessed
my very first episode of the television series *That Girl,* and I was
forever changed.

Marlo Thomas transformed my dreams. She brought to life
a universe I had never known existed—but that had been etched
indelibly into my heart. Sprawled before me was a future, possibly
my future, that I, for the first time, felt I could get excited about.
As I grew into a teenager and then entered college, I was torn between two worlds: the safe, comfortable one I knew and the risky,
exhilarating one that the faraway big city promised.

I headed west after college to pursue my big-city ambitions.
Twelve years after my adventure, I have finally established my lifelong dream of having a stable, happy home of my own—although
I've endured many struggles along the way. These sacrifices—like
working two jobs simultaneously to be able to afford to live in
Los Angeles, driving a beat-up car in a city whose residents boast
Beemers and Mercedes, sharing cramped quarters, and having
to make new friends—have made my success as an independent
woman all the sweeter.

The annoyances of sharing my space with roommates paid
off especially big when I decided to buy my own home. Sharing
rent, utilities, and furniture expenses with roommates compromised my freedom to do as I pleased in my apartment, but it also
enabled me to save money toward a down payment on my own
place, and even collect enough furniture to fill it. The time finally
came to stop playing house and start living it.

Uncertain about where to start, I began house hunting by wandering into homes in my immediate neighborhood that had OPEN HOUSE signs displayed prominently in their front yards.

THE 411

In hopes of garnering potential buyers, homeowners and their representatives host open houses that invite the public to peruse properties for sale.

At first, I'd wander in aimlessly, hopelessly overwhelmed by the notion that I could actually make an offer on a home. But those early open houses were also an opportunity for me to take inventory of what was on the market, what I could get within different price ranges, and what the "must haves" were for the place I would one day purchase. It was like speed dating.

Touring open homes, including places I thought I might be able to afford and condos I knew were completely out of my price range, became a new Sunday ritual. During one Sunday walkthrough, I met David, a nice independent realtor in his early forties. David was representing the seller of a two-bedroom unit in my Brentwood, California, neighborhood. The place was charming, but smaller than I'd hoped and, in my novice mind, overpriced. But David was friendly, and we chatted about my search and how to go about it. Before I knew it, he had agreed to take me on as a client.

THE 411

If you use a realtor to search for your home, make sure you carefully select one who knows well the area in which you want to buy. It is best if she has work contacts in that area, so that she is privy to insider information on homes about to be put on the market, and can refer you to local professionals who can help you if you find a home.

David guided me through the initial homebuying process and helped me navigate what I could afford. My credit score (which I'll explore in Chapter 9) reassured both of us that I was a viable candidate for a mortgage loan (see Chapter 4 for more information on this financial resource). Simultaneously, David scouted properties for me based on my list of deal-makers and negotiables. I breezed through some that I knew weren't right for me as soon as I entered them; in others, I grappled with whether the compromises I'd have to make would be worth the pros of buying the place. During that period, I also had my first experience with second looks and bidding wars.

THE 411

A "bidding war" is a real estate term to describe a situation in which a potential buyer unknowingly or knowingly bids on a property against one or more potential buyers, ultimately driving the price up. The highest bidder typically wins.

Nothing stuck. After two years of looking, none of the homes seemed quite right. Between looking, bidding, and passing, I grew tired. I felt defeated and disenchanted. Home prices continued to surge. The longer it took me to find the right condo, the more I had to compromise about what kind of place I could afford and get.

Even though I'd come close to purchasing a home, something invariably ruined the deal. Typically, it was during negotiations that I'd dig in my heels on principle, unwilling to go above the seller's asking price. My ego got in my way, and I realized that if I were to actually move forward and make a purchase, I would need to reconcile my heart with my head. Upon further reflection, I owned that while I wanted to buy a home, my heart simply wasn't ready for it; I was still scared of taking this leap alone. And so I did what was right for me at the time: I postponed my search for one year.

But I didn't sacrifice my dream. Instead, I gave myself that year to save up more money for a down payment. I immediately authorized my financial advisor to automatically withdraw nearly

$1,000 a month from my account and invest it in a money market account. This approach allowed me to earn more interest on my money (and prevented me from spending it foolishly), but kept it accessible so that I could make a down payment when the year ended. Simultaneously, I embraced my short-term dreams of more adventures abroad and began planning trips to France and Costa Rica.

SHAKE YOUR MONEY MAKER

Knowing where to invest your money to make the most of it is your responsibility. Read *The Hip Girl's Handbook for Home, Car & Money Stuff* and *The Hip Girl's Handbook for the Working World* to brush up on the basics of finances and benefits. Then expand your financial know-how with books like *Smart Women Finish Rich* and *The 9 Steps to Financial Freedom.* Finally, consider building a strong financial go-to team, including a financial advisor and tax accountant, to help you regularly monitor and manage your investments.

In that year, my international travels nurtured my spirit in a way that homebuying couldn't have. And I wouldn't have been able to afford such luxuries if I had taken on a mortgage payment. But because I never lost sight of my long-term goal of buying my own home in a year, I was also able to save nearly $12,000 more while allowing myself other, reasonable indulgences. Yes, I might have saved even more had I been more frugal that year—but by the end of it, I was in a better financial position to get more bang for my buck, and I'd satiated my hunger for excitement and culture.

With my heart, head, and finances aligned, I was truly ready to become a homebuyer. I embraced my new goal with unabashed fierceness and began the process all over again. This time, because I had two years' experience under my belt, my approach to the game was smarter and more calculated. Within ten days of taking a more rigorous tack, I found a place I loved that would become my new home.

three

THE "DIRTY LITTLE COSTS" OF HOMEBUYING

Down Payment, Property Taxes, and Insurance

"*A*fter attending college in the South, I headed west to see what else was out there for me," says my neighbor Amilee, a thirty-two-year-old Santa Monica resident. "I started waiting tables at a high-end steak house. Our clients were very wealthy—old-school money and new. I remember thinking, *How do I get what they have—the freedom to live my life as I choose?*

"I'm very independent, and buying my own home had always been a goal of mine," Amilee explains. "I thought maybe that would be my way into the kind of life I saw my patrons living. But housing prices were so exorbitant. The market certainly showed no signs of stabilizing, let alone slowing, and I didn't think I could possibly afford a big enough down payment to buy, let alone in the area I wanted to live in."

THE 411

A down payment is the lump sum of money a buyer applies up front toward the total purchase price of a home. The down payment is used to pay a portion of the total cost of the home, assuming a home costs more than you can afford to pay outright. Generally, you buy the rest of the home by securing a loan from a lending company. The required down payment amount varies from loan to loan, and depends on the purchase price of the home and your own financial goals.

"My boyfriend encouraged me to investigate it anyway," Amilee admits. "The time was right to buy in my life. My roommate was moving out, and to rent somewhere else was going to double my cost. So I thought, *Why not just look into how much more I'd need to save?*

"I met with a mortgage broker and I couldn't believe what I was hearing. I was astonished to learn I did have enough money to get an affordable mortgage and a home I could be proud of. And I discovered I could afford to buy in an even better neighborhood then I'd ever imagined!"

Amilee began searching for her home immediately. Her friends and manager at the restaurant where she worked thought she had her head in the clouds. "They couldn't imagine how I could do it, and were kind of Debbie Downers about it. I guess it made them feel better to put down my goals, because otherwise they might feel badly about themselves for not being able to do the same thing. I had to learn to keep my search for a home low-key. I didn't need that kind of shortsighted, negative energy around me."

After a few months of looking, Amilee found a place she liked and could afford. She pooled her tips and the small savings fund her parents had gifted her years before for the down payment on her first home. Since she was prequalified for a loan, securing a mortgage was relatively easy. And Amilee became the proud solo owner of her first home at age twenty-seven.

That was in 2002. Amilee's property has since more than doubled in value, even though she's done nothing more than paint the interior of her two-bedroom beach-city condo. Amilee feels so empowered by her feat that she has been inspired to make real estate her primary moneymaker.

Amilee stayed on as a waitress full-time for a few more years. During that time, she saved up enough of her money to purchase another condo in her home state of Florida. Now Amilee rents out her second property and earns enough to pay both her mortgages. She's been able to cut back to waitressing part-time, and is working with financial backers to fund her first apartment building. This, she hopes, will one day be her ticket to financial security and wealth.

**FIVE WAYS TO FUND A DOWN PAYMENT
(WITHOUT GETTING YOUR KNICKERS IN A WAD)**

1. Consider a cheaper home. You'll need to put less money down for it up front.

2. Borrow against retirement savings plans. For instance, different IRAs (Individual Retirement Accounts) offer an early withdrawal of up to a certain limit, without paying a penalty, for the sole purpose of purchasing your very first home.

3. Save more quickly. Spend less and invest your money in a higher-interest account.

4. Seek out loans that offer low-down-payment programs. You must have great credit to qualify. Pitfall? Be prepared to pay higher interest rates and up-front fees.

5. Look into special-situation loans. A couple of financing options to ask your mortgage broker or loan institution about are 80-10-10 and 80-15-5, which involve taking out more than one loan to cover the share you don't have a down payment for. But with less of your own money at risk up front, you'll face more fees and higher mortgage interest rates.

Collecting a down payment is your first step toward making your homebuying fantasy a reality. Just how much you should put down is the question; numerous financial and real estate experts disagree about what amount is sufficient.

Your parents' parents would be likely to heed the more historic view that a 20 percent down payment is best, and anything less is foolish. In the case of an investment like a home, would-be homeowners who have managed to save 20 percent for a down payment would definitely be considered less risky to lenders.

Putting more money down means that lenders are loaning you less money, and that you're less likely to default on the loan.

Some financial experts, meanwhile, argue that a home is really only valuable to a seller upon selling. Therefore, they advocate putting a smaller percentage down—5 to 10 percent—up front as a smarter strategy for investing. Doing so leaves you open to other opportunities that might yield a faster and possibly higher return on your investment.

In recent years, "100 percent financing" home purchases surged as loan companies offered mortgage loan packages with "teaser rates." These included adjustable rate mortgages (ARMs), which encourage people to purchase a home who otherwise couldn't afford it, or who didn't have a down payment. However, homeowners, homebuyers, and loan companies faced a backlash from the barrage of people who just "wanted to get in the game." These people overextended themselves by buying homes that were priced too high for their budgets, because loan companies were too quick to loan them more money than they could afford on a month-to-month basis. Additionally, the loans were riddled with lender fees and often designed to "get people in," but not structured for affordability for the long haul. As homeowners with ARM loans faced increasing interest rates, their budgets couldn't support the rising month-to-month cost of owning.

Inevitably, homeowners began defaulting on these inflatable loans. Attempts to sell to avoid foreclosure failed because the market had slowed (and slumped in some regions), causing many homeowners to owe more on their loan than their property was

now worth. Loan companies were forced to foreclose in hopes
of recouping their losses quickly. Having learned a harsh lesson,
most loan companies have now stopped offering 100 percent financing, leaving wannabe homeowners few options to buy without a decent down payment.

THE 411

Seller financing, otherwise called "owner will carry," is when the
seller of a home fronts you the money directly to buy their home.
This kind of financing is typically due to the seller in five to ten
years, after which point you, the buyer, must convert to a larger,
conventional loan. Such properties are difficult to find, and you
should look closely for any seller-financing red flags, like major
defects in the property itself, or inflated interest rates. Also, be sure
to hire an attorney to ensure that paperwork, including the title, is
written fairly.

With so many differing professional opinions, determining
how much of a down payment you should pay is challenging.
Consider using both the state of the mortgage market at the time
you're purchasing and your personal financial outlook as a ba-
rometer. Review your overall finances. Work with your financial
advisor and accountant to determine your long- and short-term
financial goals. Incorporate these factors, along with closing costs
(Chapter 15), taxes and insurance (Chapter 3), and maintenance

expenses (Chapter 16), when determining what kind of down payment and loan are right for you.

TWELVE REASONS TO COVER YOUR ASS

Because there are back-end expenses in homebuying that loan companies won't cover (see Chapter 15), it's a good idea to get a head start now on saving for these costs. Start by inquiring with a mortgage or escrow officer to find out approximately how much closing will cost you for a home in the price range you think you can afford. Here are twelve closing costs you need to consider (and start saving for) before you buy:

1. Recording fee: The fee charged to record the mortgage and deed. Cost is around $50.

2. Courier fees: Documents are time sensitive in order to meet deadlines in escrow (the process of closing the sale on a property). Check that these charges are kept to a minimum in your final paperwork.

3. Notary: You'll need an official to verify your signature on all the paperwork to make it legal. Notary charges can run you a couple hundred dollars or more, depending on your official agreement.

4. Escrow fees: Escrow charges vary from a few hundred dollars to thousands for handling and filing the paperwork for your new home.

5. Legal fees: These charges depend on your deal.

6. Inspections: Inspecting your house for various issues can run from a couple hundred dollars to thousands, depending on the size of the property.

7. Loan origination points and fees: Mortgage lenders charge for multiple aspects of the homebuying process, including

basic things like loan documents and pulling your credit report. They may also charge an origination fee (1 or 2 percent of the loan). You can get a loan with few or no origination fees, but at a higher interest rate.

8. Prepaid loan interest: Many lenders start accruing interest on your loan from the time your loan is funded.

9. Property taxes: This is Uncle Sam's share for your purchase, and it may cost you a couple hundred to thousands of dollars, depending on the price of your home. You may owe your seller tax-reimbursement costs for any taxes they paid in advance.

10. Title insurance: Lenders require title insurance to make sure your home is clear to be sold to you. It costs several hundred dollars or more.

11. Private mortgage insurance (PMI): If your down payment is less than 20 percent, a mortgage lender will likely require you to take out PMI in case you default on your loan. Avoid this charge when you can; otherwise, you'll be charged for several months' premiums in advance.

12. Homeowner's insurance: You need insurance to own a home if a loan institution is backing your purchase. This can cost several hundred or several thousand dollars per year, with the first year's payment required at the time of purchase.

Even if average home costs decrease over the course of a few years, over time, they're likely to increase substantially, ultimately accruing a sizable profit for you when you're ready to sell. And one of the best reasons to buy a home is the great annual tax benefit you'll receive. So even if you don't see immediate market increases in your area, be patient and consider your gains.

Generally speaking, during the first several years or so of your loan, your monthly mortgage payment is mainly to cover the interest on the actual loan. With a mortgage, you get to deduct the interest and taxes from your regular income when you file your annual income tax return. In laymen's terms, this means that the government is cutting you some slack come April fifteenth, simply for being a homeowner.

But while it's lovely to know you'll likely get a nice little "savings" from the government when you file your annual income taxes, how about scraping up the money to pay for the property taxes year-round? That, too, is quite a chunk of change. Coming up with hundreds to several thousands of dollars can be reason enough to wonder if you can, in fact, truly afford to buy a place.

You do have a choice of how to pay your property taxes. Some buyers opt to roll the cost into their monthly payment. Putting a little away monthly makes it feel like less of a hefty burden. Others, including me, choose to come up with the money when it's due. Fortunately, the government kindly alleviates its imposing annual "shakedown" with a two-installment payment option that can make the tax burden feel less overwhelming. While it's always stressful knowing you need to find the money somewhere to pay it—in my case, a whopping $7,000 a year or a two-time $3,500 installment—it's helped me feel a bit less strapped month to month.

However you choose to pay your annual property tax, work with your tax accountant before you buy to help you calculate how much you'll incur in taxes for the price range you're considering. This tactic will help you cement exactly how much house you can afford. Your tax advisor can also help you decide what you can claim as deductions toward your annual income taxes, and how your paycheck can be adjusted to make homeowning more comfortable for you in your everyday life.

THE 411

Once you're officially a homeowner, keep an eye on home prices in your area. If they drop, enlist the help of your real estate agent for homes for sale in your area that are similar in size and condition to your home. Real estate property taxes are based on the estimated value of a home. If your home's value has dropped since you've purchased it, appeal the amount of property taxes you pay. Contact your local assessor's office to contest exactly how much you pay in property taxes.

Another hidden cost of homeowning is insurance. I've mentioned it briefly above as it pertains to your mortgage, but you also need to protect yourself as a homeowner. In the event that disaster strikes, insurance protects you from losing everything you've worked so hard for.

Numerous types of insurance plans can protect your assets. Different regions call for different insurance coverage. Some places experience natural disasters like thunderstorms, tornadoes, earthquakes, and hurricanes. Others are vulnerable to mudslides and brushfires that can cause extensive damage. Household disasters can also result from accidents, like leaving your curling iron on and starting a fire. Or, heaven forbid, you could be burglarized.

YOU SNOOZE, YOU LOSE: PROTECTING YOUR ASSETS

1. Life insurance: This insurance protects any dependents who rely on your income to live on in case you pass away. There are different kinds: term life insurance and cash-value life insurance. Consult a professional insurance agent to determine what's best for you.

2. Disability insurance: This insurance protects your most valuable asset—you. In case you fall ill and can't earn an income to live, disability insurance protects your future earnings. Look into both short-term disability and long-term disability plans. Check first with your employer to see if they already pay for disability insurance on your behalf, and, if so, inquire about what their plan covers. You may need to take out a larger policy to cover your lifestyle.

3. Comprehensive health insurance: If you become ill, medical bills can consume you. You need comprehensive health insurance to help you pay these bills.

4. Regional disaster insurance: Different states will cover you for various regional catastrophes. Ask a professional insurance agent whom you trust what you need to buy for your area.

5. Homeowner's insurance: In the case of a robbery, fire, visitor injury on your property, or the like, this insurance is a must. Chances are, if you have a loan, your lender requires that you purchase this insurance.

6. Umbrella or excess liability insurance: Your homeowner and auto insurance should also include liability insurance. But as you accrue more net worth, you may want to purchase supplemental liability insurance to protect it.

The more you own, the more you need to recoup losses. Therefore, just having these insurances isn't enough if the policy you're paying for won't pay for all that you've lost. Work with your insurance agent to make sure that you're insuring yourself and your assets properly, and that the kind of policy you've selected won't make replacing them difficult. Take the highest deductible that you can afford to dish out in the event of a claim. While it may bite to dole out $500 from your own pocket, it will help keep the overall cost of your coverage lower.

Adding all of these extraneous, but necessary, costs to your bottom dollar will help you make a more informed decision about what you can actually afford to pay toward a home. While I am a huge proponent of buying a home on your own, I think it's equally important to enjoy your life. Not factoring in the additional costs of a down payment, tax, insurance, and maintenance (Chapter 3) could really cramp your style. You might believe you can afford your home, but if that means slashing your budget for important life experiences, like traveling, socializing, and the occasional new outfit, you may want to rethink your finances. Fortunately, I found experienced and educated real estate professionals to help me navigate the homebuying process. Otherwise, I could have easily been surprised by and faced financial ruin upon purchasing my first home.

four

The Who, Where, What, and Why of
Mortgage Loan Packages, Brokers, and Agents

*A*ll the relationships in my life have been packed with pas-
sion, pitfalls, fear, and life lessons—including my relationship with money.

Money is just like a good girlfriend. We've had our ups and
downs. She's seen me through rough times, like when I broke up
with my ex-boyfriend. Money, you see, consoled me. She helped
me get a closet full of new clothes. She filled the void left in my
heart and distracted me with shopping trips, massages, and fabu-
lous dining with friends. She temporarily made me feel beautiful,
and injected occasional and much-needed doses of what felt like
happiness, even if only the elusive, materialistic kind.

Money has also left me panic-stricken about my very sur-
vival. She's caused rifts in my other relationships and taunted me
with her glittering promise of freedom—freedom to not worry
about whether I can pay my bills month to month, freedom to

partner with someone because I want to and not because I need to, freedom to explore dreams of travel or new career paths, freedom to live my life as I choose. At times, though, she's held me hostage to professional mediocrity with her promise of constant companionship.

THE 411

Being "house-poor" means a homeowner can just cover her mortgage payment but is nearly depleted of funds for doing anything else. Oftentimes, house-poor homeowners can't even afford furniture to fill their houses, let alone social outings, travel, and other recreational activities.

Money, as it turns out, was also one of the paralyzing forces that kept me from buying a home sooner. I questioned whether I could really afford it. Was money always going to be there for me come mortgage time, or when property taxes were due . . . and what if a major plumbing catastrophe occurred? If money wasn't there, who would be?

Turns out, I'm not the only one who feels this way. Lots of women say they are afraid that even if they can afford to buy a home, they won't be able to carry a mortgage on their own for the long haul. What if they lose their job or fall ill?

Many women I talk to are scared that homeowning might make them house-poor. They fear being left without excess money to do other things they enjoy, and they feel nervous about the idea of being stuck at home, alone. And then what? How will they ever meet someone if they never go out?

The prevailing question is: Exactly how much house can you afford to buy, and how does that translate in your monthly budget? First things first: If your credit score is good (see Chapter 9), you'll likely be a candidate for a good mortgage. Conversely, if your credit history is riddled with late payments, a foreclosure, bankruptcy, and other financial problems, getting a mortgage—particularly a good one—will be more challenging.

With all this talk about mortgages, let's start by clarifying exactly what one is: A mortgage is a loan you take out to pay for the portion of a home that you don't have the money for. For example, let's say a home costs $250,000. You have $50,000 saved, most of which you'll use to cover both your down payment and your closing costs. Let's say your closing costs will be just less than $5,000 (see Chapter 15). Because you're not allowed to withdraw either this fee or a down payment from your mortgage, you'll want to set aside $5,000 of your saved money to cover the costs of closing on the property. You decide you want to put $40,000 toward a down payment. That leaves an additional $210,000 to pay for the remainder of the house. You will need to secure a loan to pay the seller that amount. The money you owe is your mortgage. The process of paying on your loan, reducing your balance over time, is called amortizing the mortgage.

THE 411

Home sales over the last several years have enticed potential buyers with affordable up-front costs through interest-only loans. With these loans, a homeowner's monthly mortgage payment goes toward paying the interest on the loan, but not toward the principal balance of the overall cost of the home. Because of this loan's lower entrance barriers, many homebuyers overextend their price limitations. When these higher-risk clients then default, lenders themselves are overextended, and end up retreating from offering these types of loans, making them harder to come by.

"When I was determining if I could even conceivably afford to buy a home, I worked with a mortgage broker to find out how much I would qualify for," says Staci, a thirty-six-year-old communications executive. "I was shocked at just how much lenders were willing to loan me. Of course it made me feel great! It felt like someone else, a financial expert, really believed in me and my capability, even more than I did. And that was really reassuring," Staci confides. "Then I broke it down to a monthly payment. Boy, was that a rude awakening! I couldn't believe how, if I took out the kind of loan I qualified for, I'd really be cutting it close. Too close, to be honest, and I'd be miserable and stressed. It was comforting to know, though," Staci adds, "that if I needed the money, it was available to me."

THE "PITI" OF A MORTGAGE

1. Principal: the exact amount you owe on your loan.

2. Interest: the amount of money you're charged for borrowing money.

3. Taxes: as in property taxes, as discussed in Chapter 3. Some homebuyers opt to not include this in their monthly payment, and instead pay it in lump sums as it becomes due.

4. Insurance: A loan company will likely require you to take out private mortgage insurance (PMI) if your down payment is less than 20 percent.

Lending institutions look at several variables to determine how much money to loan a prospective buyer. These factors include your gross income (that's before taxes and any retirement monies are withdrawn), your credit score (see Chapter 9), and your reportable debt. Your debt includes anything from car payments to credit cards to school loans.

A loan company computes your income-to-debt ratio to determine how much home you can afford and how much they presume you can afford to pay toward a loan. The rules fluctuate with the times and between loan institutions, but a general rule of thumb in the industry is that a homeowner shouldn't spend much over a third of her gross income on her monthly mortgage.

LIFESTYLES OF THE SAVVY SINGLE WOMAN

Many online mortgage calculators, and even some loan companies, will qualify you for a loan beyond your means. Don't let it fool
you; stick with an amount that's comfortable for you. Remember,
only you know the kind of lifestyle you need to have to be content,
and no impersonal calculator can factor in your personal, day-to-
day happiness.

Do your own math before deciding how much loan you can
cover in a monthly mortgage payment. Don't forget to factor into
your monthly mortgage payment the interest you'll be charged for
the loan itself—this, after all, is the reason a lender is loaning you
money in the first place.

Interest rates, the rate at which a lender will loan you money,
are like a roller coaster. There are periods, even days, when they
may peak. Other times, they may dip slightly or even drop dramatically. Sometimes they will hold relatively stable over long periods of time. They are both ever-changing and a constant.

Lock yourself into a loan when interest rates have dropped
substantially. It will help you afford more home for your money.
And because interest rates fluctuate, until you have secured the
deal with a lender, the interest rate you were quoted yesterday
may have already changed. That change could mean a substantial
difference, either positive or negative, in your monthly mortgage
payment.

THE 411

Currently, a low interest rate is anywhere in the high 4 percent to low 6 percent range. Like fluctuating gas prices, even the slightest change—like half a point—can mean a difference of several thousand dollars in your overall cost of buying a home.

I can remember feeling dizzy and overwhelmed about all the mortgage information I was forced to consume when I was debating buying a home. There are so many things to consider, including one of the most important decisions regarding securing a mortgage: what kind?

Let's start with fixed versus adjustable mortgage loans. A fixed-rate mortgage doesn't vary with the market, so it allows you to budget your monthly expenses precisely. If you don't get a fixed-rate loan and you face the onset of a higher interest rate, your monthly mortgage could increase by a few or hundreds of dollars, depending on the home's interest rate and price.

Fixed-rate loans do have drawbacks that should factor in your decision making. For instance, the longer you want to lock in a loan (say, thirty years), the higher the interest rate a lender will charge you. Another thing to keep in mind is that what goes up might also come down: Interest rates may drop below your locked-in rate. If you don't qualify for refinancing (see Chapter 18), you could be missing out on substantial savings.

Another thing to be conscious of is that fixed-rate mortgages often come with prepayment penalties for paying the mortgage off early. Despite the penalty charge, these loans can be appealing to homebuyers because they often promise "no points" loans (see the sidebar below).

Now, depending on your homeowning plan, a prepayment penalty may not affect you, and a no-points loan may be suitable. But life is full of surprises, and if you have to sell before you anticipated, you could end up spending thousands of dollars in penalties just to pay off your loan.

WHAT'S THE "POINT"?

In the mortgage business, "points" are defined by the rates of interest your lender charges you for her work. Processing and approving your loan require various time-consuming tasks, like pulling your credit, appraising the property, and preparing loan documents, for which your lender may charge you a point or more. One point equals one percent of the total loan amount. Points are due at close of escrow and are tax deductible. Some lenders will tack on various other fees. One popular one is for originating the loan. If you don't plan on moving for a while, paying for a point or two and some of these other fees may be worthwhile—but only if they're attached to a low interest rate. Conversely, if you're purchasing a transitional home and cash is limited, no points and limited fees will be more beneficial to you. Just review all the fees and points carefully. You might be able to negotiate some of them.

An adjustable-rate mortgage (ARM) loan fluctuates as the market fluctuates. So if the interest rate market is on the rise, your monthly mortgage payment will be, too. However, the reverse is also true. If interest rates decrease, your monthly mortgage payment and your overall ARM interest rate on your loan decrease.

ARM loans are offered in three time frames: one year, three years, and five years. Each ARM loan adjusts at the end of the corresponding period (a three-year ARM adjusts after three years). ARM loans generally have lower interest rates than a long-term, fixed loan. For this reason, ARM loans are attractive, especially to transitional homebuyers.

Remember Staci, who was shocked by how much lenders were willing to loan her? She also felt disoriented by all the mortgage information being thrown her way. She remembers, "I was just doing some preliminary investigating, and all these questions started flying at me: How long did I plan to live in my home? What kind of loan did I want? How much did I have for a down payment? What was my housebuying limit? Did I want a fixed loan, ARM, or hybrid? Perhaps I was even a good candidate for a balloon loan. I wanted to drop the phone and run! I had little idea about what all this mortgage talk meant. I felt way in over my head!"

THE 411

Bankers often cap adjustments in ARM loans. Periodic adjustment caps limit the maximum increase and decrease of the rate change. The adjustment cap is usually 1 to 2 percent (within a one-year interval). "Lifetime caps" limit the highest rate allowed over the entire life of the loan (usually no more than 5–6 percent higher than the starting rate). Don't take on an ARM loan without a lifetime cap. Sometimes ARMs may cap the increase of your monthly payment, but not the increase of the interest rate. Bottom line? Know exactly what the terms of your loan are before signing on the dotted line.

In addition to the more traditional types of loans—fixed loans and ARMs—there is another nontraditional, but increasingly popular, loan type that's especially appealing to single women: the hybrid loan.

A hybrid loan is exactly what it sounds like: a mix between fixed-rate and adjustable-rate loans. Usually, hybrid loans begin as fixed-rate loans, but with shorter terms of three, five, or seven years. Depending on the hybrid loan you secure, it will transition into either a convertible or nonconvertible loan.

THE 411

A convertible loan becomes fixed at the current market percentage. A nonconvertible loan is an adjustable loan that fluctuates annually.

Hybrid loans are very appealing for many single women who are skeptical about locking themselves into a long-term deal solo. They're especially attractive because they're generally lower in percentage points than longer, more traditional loans, so they make homebuying more affordable. But because hybrid loan terms are longer than those of basic ARM loans, hybrid loans have higher initial interest rates than regular ARM loans do.

NONTRADITIONAL LOANS FOR THE NONTRADITIONAL GIRL

1. A balloon loan is a fixed-interest-rate loan for five, seven, or ten years. Because you pay only the interest of your loan during its term, you're indebted to pay off the entire balance of the loan when it ends.

2. Owner will carry (OWC) loans, as described in Chapter 3, involve the seller's loaning you the money directly to purchase your house within a certain time limit, generally no more than five to seven years, before transitioning to a more traditional loan. These loans are harder to find. Properties offering OWC need to be evaluated closely for hidden and

costly defects. Meanwhile, OWC contracts need to be reviewed closely by an attorney to ensure that interest rates aren't inflated.

3. Veteran's assistance (VA) loans help veterans to qualify for home financing. If you're a vet, investigate this perk as a viable option.

4. Lease-with-option loans are those in which you, the buyer, agree to buy your home for a certain price, but also agree to rent the home for a specified amount of time on the condition that the entire rent be applied toward paying down the home's overall purchase price. If the value increases over the course of the time frame you agree upon, you pay only the price that was originally set. However, if the value decreases, you aren't required to buy. Down payments for these purchases are heftier than most, and you do lose your year's investment if you back out.

5. Government assistance agencies like the Federal Housing Agency (FHA) and the U.S. Department of Housing Under Development (HUD) help secure loans for qualifying candidates who might otherwise not be in a position to buy a home by insuring lenders against potential loss. These organizations carry very specific criteria, and candidates must agree to certain restrictions. Contact HUD directly at www. hud.gov to find out more.

6. Fannie Mae and Freddie Mac are two popular government-sponsored organizations that underwrite many loans nationwide. They also offer loans to credit-challenged candidates or people who qualify for their low- or no-money-down programs, which are particularly inviting for first-time homebuyers. These loans generally come with higher interest rates, which may decrease as you pay your mortgage on time. Check out www.fanniemae.com, www.freddiemac.com, or www.homepath.com for details.

Now that you understand the ins and outs of the most recognizable mortgage loan options, you also need to consider the life of the loan before deciding which type of mortgage loan to go with. Deciding on a loan type and length is not unlike the "Which came first, the chicken or the egg?" quandary. One affects the other, and it's easy to make arguments for and against any type of loan. Different loans come with different terms, from three to five, seven, ten, fifteen, or even thirty or forty years. Each loan and loan term has varying perks and consequences. Answer some basic questions about your homebuying intentions, and then review the types of loans above to help you determine how long you should take out your loan for.

**FIVE BASIC QUESTIONS TO ASK YOURSELF
BEFORE DETERMINING YOUR LOAN LENGTH**

1. How long do I expect to live in my home?
2. Do I have a sufficient amount of money in my reserve account?
3. How much is making a monthly mortgage payment going to affect my lifestyle or paying down other debt?
4. How will I save up to pay for my property taxes if I don't roll them into my monthly mortgage payment?
5. How have interest rates and the housing market fluctuated over the past several years?

With information comes power. Hopefully now you can feel more certain when deciding on the right mortgage for you. These concepts should simply help you interpret what many homebuyers feel is an overabundance of information, and give you an overview of options and terminology. For a more thorough explanation of mortgages, refer to the Resources section at the back of this book and enlist the help of mortgage professionals.

Mortgage lenders, banks, and reputable mortgage brokers are the usual suspects to whom new and returning homebuyers turn when finding, applying for, and securing loans. Where to begin your search for a loan depends on you, on how much time you can dedicate to research, on how hands-on you prefer to be, and on how comfortable you are figuring out mortgage jargon.

If you like the thrill of the hunt and have the time and energy to do thorough research, you can locate and secure a loan all on your own. Mortgage bankers, banks, and savings and loan associations are plentiful. Look in your local phone book or online to start. Remember, as in all good negotiations, taking time to meet with potential lenders in person whenever possible, and getting competitive offers, may be the keys to your success for securing the best deal around.

Reputable online mortgage hubs make investigating and understanding loans relatively easy. Avoid the generic mortgage calculators on these sites; because so many personal variables factors into homebuying, these calculators don't provide an accurate picture of how much home you can afford. Another warning: Lenders and other home-related services and vendors pay to advertise on websites but aren't endorsed by the websites themselves.

Lastly, exercise extreme caution before agreeing to any language that contractually binds you to a real estate agency or mortgage broker. You don't want to end up tied to a company and paying them a commission just to review their listings or lender options.

Mortgage bankers serve two purposes: They find a good loan package within their network, and they directly service and close your loan for you. Financial companies like banks and savings and loan institutions are most noted for this benefit. Mortgage bankers make their money through points and fees for originating the loan, and for the work of accessing, completing, and filing all necessary paperwork. A mortgage banker can also potentially make a good amount of money after closing on the loan by selling the loan to a secondary lender at a higher percentage rate. One red flag: Because mortgage bankers are intimately involved in the actual lending process, they may be too invested to get you the best deal possible. Consider enlisting the help of a mortgage broker.

A mortgage broker is an independent contractor or representative of a company who acts as a sort of dating service, matching borrowers with lenders of home loans. Mortgage brokers also do all the paperwork, including applying for the loan and processing and filing documents, to help you secure the right loan package. Unlike mortgage bankers, mortgage brokers don't service the loan, so they can't sell it to a secondary lender to make even more money off of the sale. However, sometimes your mortgage banker will work extra hard to secure you an attractive loan package if you've been a good, long-term client. If you've got the time, why limit your options? Check into both.

REPUTABLE ONLINE MORTGAGE RESOURCES

1. HSH Associates (www.hsh.com) is a wealth of knowledge regarding all things mortgage related. It offers up-to-date information, including fluctuating interest rates, loan options, and resources and articles on homebuying issues.

2. E-loan (www.eloan.com) is a reputable, mortgage-specific website boasting a cornucopia of loans from numerous lenders. It also offers loan consultants through a toll-free number and allows you to track pending loan offers.

3. Fannie Mae or Freddie Mac (www.homepath.com), as noted earlier, are quasi-public, government-monitored organizations. They both offer loans to potential homebuyers in a number of capacities, as well as some explanations of basic mortgage and homebuying jargon and processes.

4. Long-standing local and nationwide financial institutions, lenders, and insurance companies like Prudential and Bank of America can gauge what's available to you. Don't rely on just one company, though; make sure to shop around.

Reputable mortgage brokers have strong relationships with a plethora of mortgage lenders who are specifically interested in originating loans for potential homebuyers. Most mortgage brokers will charge you a fee of 0.5 to 2 percent of the total loan value for their services. These points are competitive with the points and fees a mortgage banker or lender will charge you. However, a mortgage broker may negotiate a lower commission to enlist you as a client, which means savings for you, and for little work! When negotiating, keep in mind that mortgage brokers don't get paid unless the deal is completed. So it's in their best interest to work hard for your money and compile a mortgage package that's appealing to you.

Ask trusted friends, colleagues, and family members for mortgage broker referrals. Your real estate agent will also likely have a bevy of mortgage broker resources to offer. But don't pick someone just because your best friend liked them. You need someone whose work style and resources cater to your specific needs. And always talk to several before selecting the best broker for you.

TEN QUESTIONS TO ASK YOUR POTENTIAL MORTGAGE BROKER

1. What is their success rate for marrying lenders with borrowers?

2. How do they prefer to communicate with their clients—by phone, by email, or in person? Does their answer work with your communication preference?

3. How many clients are they currently courting? You need to be a priority, especially considering that mortgage loans come with deadlines.

4. How big is their talent pool of lenders? The more lenders they work with, the better chance you have of securing the best deal out there.

5. Do they participate in professional mortgage associations and ongoing educational seminars? If so, how frequently? Like a hairdresser, you want a mortgage broker who's on top of the latest trends and options in mortgage loans, and who has the contacts to make it happen.

6. Do they work with candidates who have a down payment that's less than 20 percent? This criterion is critical if you're

planning on putting down less than 20 percent, as you don't want to waste your time.

7. How long have they been in business?

8. What do they normally charge for their commission?

9. If they're local, can you meet them in person? This person will have access to a lot of your personal information. They shouldn't hesitate to invite you to their office for a formal meet-and-greet.

10. Questions to ask yourself: Do you like their personal style? Are they straightforward, and can they talk to you in laymen's terms? Do they take time to explain something you don't understand? Do they give you more information than you can stand? Do you feel confident that they know their stuff, or does your gut tell you to call their bluff? Do you sense they're detail oriented? Loans aren't scenarios in which minor restrictions and requirements can be overlooked.

Even if a potential mortgage broker answers these questions satisfactorily, and even if her fees are similar to or less than a lender or mortgage banker's, other deterrents may persuade you not to hire a mortgage broker. For example, some lenders don't market to mortgage brokers. This could mean that an even better deal is yours for the taking, but you'll need to do the research to find it. Also, some mortgage brokers may charge a larger commission than if you'd gone directly to a lender for the loan. Inquire how much commission they're making from securing the loan, then don't be afraid to negotiate their commission. It's not only in your best interest—it's your right as a potential client.

Finding the right kind of loan for your first home is an important step. It will likely play a key role in the experience you have as a homebuyer, and will affect how you feel overall when purchasing your next home. Ultimately, it's like raising a child: No matter how much research and reading you do, nothing can fully prepare you until you go through the experience yourself. Deciding on a mortgage can be extremely nerve-racking. After all, it's going to affect your finances and quality of life!

Once I'd done the work of finding a couple of reputable mortgage brokers whom friends referred, I carefully reviewed their best loan options for my case. I then reached out to friends and family members for any other personal contacts they knew. I ended up getting in touch with John, a friend of my mom's. He had worked in the mortgage business in the Midwest, and he offered to review the loan options for me as a favor. Through several emails and phone calls, John made sure that I fully understood the terms of my choices and reassured me that I wasn't being taken for a ride, no matter what package I selected.

John was an angel of reason and comfort. And just knowing I had an expert in my corner, a person who was not affected by or invested in my decision, was just the nudge I needed to take the proverbial plunge. And I haven't looked back since.

ﬁve

At a recent barbecue in Venice Beach, Calif.—a diverse area that attracts a hodgepodge of tourists, bohemian surfers, up-and-coming artists, and celebrities by day and a mix of gang members, homeless people, and bar-hopping hipsters by night— I met Susan, a woman in her late twenties who had recently moved to Los Angeles from Kansas. Probably because we shared Midwestern roots, I took to Susan immediately.

Susan had moved to Los Angeles a year prior and initially settled in West Hollywood. Sight unseen, Susan had chosen West Hollywood because acquaintances had told her that it was a cool place to live, in the center of all things fun in L.A. So she found an apartment online before even seeing it in person. Within two months, Susan was ready to get out of the neighborhood. The West Hollywood scene, which is very colorful, loud, and urban-trendy, was too much for her. Susan missed open spaces and a certain mellowness that West Hollywood simply doesn't offer. After learning about a few other neighborhoods in the Los Angeles area, Susan moved to the Valley. "And I love it!" she proclaimed.

Many single swingers in their twenties and thirties who live in Los Angeles proper often buy in the suburbs of the Valley because they're priced out of the trendier, more urban areas. But for Susan, the suburban lifestyle reminded her of home and felt comforting. She was able to get a dog. She had a backyard and could afford more space for her dime. And, most important, she slept soundly at night in quiet and safety. The Valley was her idea of home, the place where she felt most like herself. She felt it was worth the forty-minute commute to her job every day because of all those factors.

When I first moved to Los Angeles, I lived in the Valley, too. It didn't fit me at all. I eventually moved to several other areas before determining that the Westside was the best fit for me, at least while I'm young and single. But it took those years of renting and trying out different areas of Los Angeles to help me figure that out. It was like dating: If you've been doing it long enough, it only takes a date or two—or, in some cases, five minutes—to know whether you're going to want to spend more time with that person. My apartment "little black book," filled with multiple penciled-in addresses, illustrated my history of neighborhood courting. It was the courting, though, that ultimately enabled me to narrow my homebuying search to one specific area: the Westside.

The Westside was where I had made my life. My core group of girlfriends—my support system and companionship in this otherwise isolating city—all lived on the Westside. My job was on the

Westside, and so was my nature-loving soul. I knew where Susan was coming from: It's important to find the place that feels like home, especially in our twenties and thirties (or sometimes even later), when many of us are still trying to figure out who we are and where we belong.

I chose the Westside because it's nestled between the beach and the majestic mountainside. I was also drawn to the array of characters that the Westside houses amid several neighborhoods with hefty home prices. Buying in such a coveted area practically guaranteed that my property would at least maintain its value over time, and would more likely increase. While buying in a neighborhood that inspired me was my priority, owning in one that sustained its worth was critical to my financial stability. And so I weighed both factors heavily when deciding where to live.

THE 411

Experts agree location is the most critical factor affecting a home's value. When choosing where to live, be sure to consider the neighborhood's value over time. Established and well-maintained neighborhoods will be more expensive, but will likely keep their worth. Riskier yet promising areas that are not yet fully developed are more affordable. Just be sure to look for positive signs that the area will in fact boom, including sprouting businesses, home sales, and city plans for parks, schools, hospitals, and more businesses.

During the first couple of years of my exploration, I embraced the entire Westside area. By keeping my options broad but focused enough, I increased my chances of finding a condo in an area I could both live in and afford. After numerous drive-bys and ride-alongs with my then-realtor, I found my first would-be home in Bel-Air.

Bel-Air is an affluent gated community on the outskirts of the UCLA community that's tucked safely among hills lush with groomed greenery. It's beautiful, peaceful, safe, and family friendly. It was also just a twenty-minute jaunt to my work, my girlfriends, and the hot spots in Santa Monica.

Bel-Air balanced my deal-makers and my negotiables. My little Bel-Air beauty was an adorable two-bedroom, nine hundred–square-foot box with a fireplace and a community pool, all encapsulated within a well-maintained building in a nice location. Oh, and I could afford it. So, after test-driving the neighborhood during different times of day, going to and from my work during peak traffic hours and on weekends, I decided to place an offer.

I didn't end up getting that Bel-Air home. I lost it to another buyer after becoming embroiled in a bidding war. Initially, my ego was bruised. I wasn't heartbroken, but I was disappointed. I questioned whether I would ever find another place that fit my criteria, and one that I could call mine for the long haul.

I continued walk-throughs of several other properties over the next few weeks, and I discovered quickly that losing the Bel-Air property had been a blessing in disguise. While it was appealing in many ways, in retrospect I realized that I would have felt isolated living there, alienated from my friends and a happening social life. No property could compensate for my longing for companionship. I needed to be around my friends, local hangouts, and an environment that still presented the possibility of meeting my Mr. Right.

KNOW WHAT YOU NEED

1. How safe is the neighborhood? Check out police reports and the general reputation of the area through word of mouth. Drive the neighborhood during the day and in the evening.

2. How long would your commute to work be? How congested is it with traffic?

3. If you're a single mom, is quality, affordable schooling nearby? How about places for kids to play safely? Are there other families, or mainly singles, nearby?

4. Are modern conveniences and public facilities nearby, like grocery stores, hospitals, police stations, shops, and restaurants?

5. Is there space for a pet to play, both inside and out?

6. Will you be able to realistically afford a home in the neighborhood, incorporating monthly utility costs?

7. Is the neighborhood bustling or peaceful, day and night?

8. Are any new business-development plans in the works for the area? Check with the city's zoning and planning divisions.

9. Are there primarily residential, freestanding single-family homes, co-ops/condos, or apartments, or a mix thereof?

10. Are there parks and recreation areas?

11. What's the history of property values in the area? Are there a lot of FOR SALE signs posted in the neighborhood? If so, find

out why. Also find out, through your realtor or a real estate website, how long some of the homes have been on the market, and whether home prices have been lowered to sell.

12. Will you have a nearby support system—friends, family, or otherwise?

13. How is the curbside appeal (a real estate term used to describe a structure and property's appearance from the outside) of the general neighborhood? Are the homes and apartment complexes well maintained? Is the surrounding landscape attractive?

WRITE YOUR PERSONAL-AD WISH LIST

List your own priorities here:

_____

_____

_____

_____

_____

_____

_____

_____

_____

_____

six

ARE YOU LOW- OR HIGH-MAINTENANCE?

Choosing Between Shared Living and a
Freestanding Single-Family Home

y good friend Tina's mom is in a predicament that she
could have never fathomed thirty years ago when she im-
migrated to the United States with her husband in their early, ide-
alistic twenties. At that time, drunk on love for her new husband,
she relinquished all household and financial decision making
to him.

Though Ann always worked and is sufficiently skilled in com-
puters and general office tasks, she never questioned her husband's
control over their financial future. He was the breadwinner. It
was just easiest that way. Now, two grown kids later, Ann is getting a divorce and is faced with establishing her own identity. She
has neither credit nor a separate savings fund. But all is not lost; at
least she has a clean canvas on which to paint her future.

Now in her early fifties, Ann is newly single, newly responsible for budgeting her monthly expenses, and newly on the

65

market for buying a home solo. The idea is empowering and exciting, yet quite overwhelming. The divorce did not leave her penniless or hopeless, but it certainly did not offer her the financial reward that Charlotte from *Sex and the City* reaped when she and Trey called it quits. Ann would not be gifted an uptown million-dollar flat, or be able to pawn a half-million-dollar engagement diamond and china for a down payment on a property of her own.

Ann rightfully received half the dividends from the sale of the couple's home, as well as some from other long-term financial investments. But in today's real estate market, whether it's precarious or stable, buying a home—never mind the home of your dreams—is very difficult. And in Ann's case, she wasn't thinking only about herself. Her eighteen-year-old son would still be living with her while he determined what to do with his career and future over the next four or five years.

Ann worried about whether she could pull off a monthly mortgage all on her own, and in a location she desired. Would she have enough money for a down payment on a home that was big enough for her and her son? What about unpredictable emergencies: plumbing, sickness, or job loss? Buying her own home would be financially draining as it was; would she be capable of overcoming the other inevitable obstacles life sets up for us?

Single women in their late twenties to early forties are not so different from newly single women in their fifties, sixties, and beyond, after all. As Ann relayed her story to me, I found myself relating to much of what she was going through. I had been in the same vulnerable position as she was. Our situations had manifested themselves differently, but our concerns about whether we could afford to buy a home were similar. Neither Ann nor I dreamed that our yellow-brick-road homebuying journeys would happen solo. Ann had already lived the so-called American dream, with the husband, children, and career, in a nice, single-family suburban home replete with a backyard and a bedroom for each of her children to call their own.

Given her financial situation, Ann's house hunt was quite a different story. Her vision of "perfection" was unattainable, unrealistic, at least for now. Aside from the financial burden of owning a single-family home in San Diego County, she needed to consider a multitude of other factors. A yard would be costly, and she'd have to take care of it by herself. A sizable home would mean more cleaning. It would also increase the likelihood that things would need fixing, things that she couldn't do on her own, like painting the exterior, roofing, plumbing, and so on. Overall, a stand-alone home would require more of her attention, more work, and more financial resources than what Ann had to give at the time. As a result, she would have to consider purchasing a condominium.

Like Ann's, my childhood fairytale of living happily ever after in a quaint, freestanding single-family home surrounded by a small, fenced-in yard amid a charming, tree-lined neighborhood would have to wait. Life had presented me with a different plan. While my circumstances varied from Ann's—I had a lifetime of good credit as reassurance, and Ann's needs in a home were different—our paths had landed us at the same intersection: buying a home as single women. Because the exorbitant cost of houses

makes homebuying with one income challenging, both Ann and I
would have to accept that all we could afford on our salaries was
a condo. And as it turned out, that circumstance proved more
advantageous that either of us could have predicted.

THE 411

Condominiums (condos) and co-ops are "attached" or "shared"
living spaces. With condos, you singularly own the interior walls
of your unit and everything within it. You also share equal ownership and maintenance expenses for all exterior portions with the
other homeowners in your complex. You pay a preset but fluid
homeowner's fee every month for the upkeep of the complex, including such services as garbage collection, janitorial, and landscaping; insurance; legal fees; and property management.

Conversely, co-ops, though often similar in appearance to condos,
are set up differently in terms of ownership and responsibilities.
Rather than owning the walls and everything within them like you
do in a condo, in a co-op, you're buying into a corporation. Your
monthly mortgage payment gives you a percentage of ownership in
the company that owns your building. The more space you own in
the building, the more shares you own, and the more you therefore
owe in monthly maintenance charges and any overall expenses.
On the other hand, owning more shares means you have more say
in overall decisions for your building.

Sure, condominium living wouldn't necessarily afford me all the liberties and benefits that a freestanding single-family home includes. Decisions like installing a skylight, a washer and dryer, hardwood floors, or a satellite dish, or even having pets, would require petitioning my homeowners' association's board of directors. It also meant I wouldn't have as much privacy, or a backyard for sunbathing and barbecuing. But it also didn't give me all the responsibilities that come with owning a private home. The fact that the homeowners' association dues would be covering massive expenses, like plumbing, painting, retrofitting the building, landscaping, and utilities, would enable me to afford a home in a location I wanted to live in. Ultimately, my starter-home reality turned out to be a cozy and freshly remodeled two-bedroom, thousand-square-foot condo in a well-maintained, sixty-nine-unit complex.

As for Ann, she opted to downsize and recently entered into escrow (defined more thoroughly in Chapter 15) on her very first two-bedroom, singly purchased condo just outside of San Diego. Ann was able to find a relatively affordable place, and spending less money left her with a "rainy day" fund that comforted her during this uncertain time in her life. It also meant she would share the responsibilities of repairing a leaky roof or structural damage, and daily expenses like garbage pickup, landscaping, and water bills, with other condo owners. She would be neither alone nor fully responsible in the face of hardship or catastrophe. And since it had less space to fill, a condo was the right choice. It didn't feel quite so empty, and Ann was able to keep up with its daily maintenance. Ultimately, buying a condo felt like the best and safest decision.

KNOW THE RULES OF ENGAGEMENT

Before buying a condo or into a co-op, carefully read the CC&Rs (the declaration of covenants, conditions, and restrictions), and any association's rules and regulations handbook, as these documents dictate your rights to nearly everything, from pet ownership to remodeling, FOR SALE signage to subletting. It's also critical to review the financials of your shared property, both its monthly operating budget and especially its reserve account (which should reflect a sizable sum of money in case of big-ticket expenses).

In some areas of the country, it's surprisingly financially feasible for single women to purchase a private home. But don't let the extra space and privacy be your only decision-making factors. Be sure to ask yourself pertinent lifestyle questions that will help you determine if a (and which kind of) freestanding single-family home is right for you:

1. Will you be home to maintain the space, interior, and grounds? And will this extra space cost you more to maintain it?

2. Can you afford the additional costs of monthly maintenance or emergencies in a private home?

3. Do you have the money, patience, and resources to remodel?

4. Can you cover the appropriate amount of insurance on your property?

5. Will you feel safe living alone in your neighborhood?

6. How long to do plan to live there, and could you rent out part of your home to cover your monthly mortgage should you need to?

Asking yourself these lifestyle questions is key in helping you determine what the right kind of property is for you to buy. If time, travel, and construction skills are not in your favor, you might consider a freestanding single-family property that's either newly built or freshly remodeled. Conversely, if your time is flexible and you're planning to stay in your home for the long run, a "fixer-upper" could be calling your name. You will get the property for less money, but at the expense of more of your time, financial resources, conveniences, and sweat.

seven

DIAMOND IN THE ROUGH OR WELL GROOMED?

Prioritizing Your Home's Interior and Exterior Wardrobes

I hold certain childhood memories near and dear to my heart: memories tied to events in homes, rooms, and backyards; memories I hope to be able to re-create for my own kids one day. Like the time my clever brothers and sisters and I strung fishing lines across the backyard from my sister's bedroom window to our neighbor Staci's bedroom window.

The whole scheme started because we had a curfew on using the phone. But even after a long day of playing, we weren't ready for the fun to end. We decided it would be cool if we could beat "the system."

This was at the peak of invention-television programs like *MacGyver* and *Remington Steele*. So we dug through our sheds, looking for a mechanism that could help us communicate late into the evening, past our bedtimes. There, among the masses of nails and shovels and lawn mowers, we discovered fishing line. With its

thin, waxlike, resilient material, it was the perfect tool for trans-
mitting our late-night shenanigans.

My brothers and sisters and I threw the roll of fishing line
from our second-story window and watched it fall quickly to the
ground. Then we ran it up through Staci's house from her second-
floor bedroom. We repeated the cycle until we had a fully func-
tioning rotating "skyline." This, we determined, was the most
genius idea *ever!*

It was time to put our messenger system to the test. We
scrounged up a handful of clothespins and scribbled some parent-
unapproved joke on spiral paper before clipping it firmly to the
fishing line. Slowly and carefully, we shimmied the line, sending
the paper from our bedroom to Staci's. And what do you know?
It worked! We'd successfully outsmarted our parents and were
breaking all the rules. We were so proud.

I look back on those times now and appreciate them even
more. My brothers and sisters and I share a lot of stories in that
old house—some good and others I'd rather forget altogether. By
the time I began my house hunt, I was ready to create new stories.
I wanted a home that could tell the tale of my next journey, filled
with old friends, new neighbors, and—who knew?—perhaps even
a new love or two.

I wanted a place that suited the life space I was in. My home
would need to be a place I could be proud of, where I could invite friends and families over for dinner parties, despite the reality
that I'd rarely ventured anywhere near the kitchen in my former
apartment. I was at a turning point in my life, on a new path,

and I wanted a home that reflected who I was and who I was becoming—not where I'd been.

That meant I would need to figure out "who" that was and how that translated into a home. As in job hunting, identifying my most important priorities in my house hunt would save me time and money. I could always negotiate later on the items that didn't matter quite as much.

DREAM BIG

Flip through home-related structural and decorating magazines to whet your palate. Magazines like *Domino, Architectural Digest, O, Midwest Living,* and *Better Homes and Gardens* all feature homes and rooms that might help you visualize your dream home. Watch HGTV (Home & Garden Television) for a multitude of programs that service all sorts of home remodeling, selling, buying, and decorating ideas. Do walk-throughs of do-it-yourself home stores like the Home Depot, Lowe's, and Sears, and of for-sale properties, even those above your price range. Your goal is to see as many different options as possible to assist you in figuring out your preferences. Even if you can't afford a sprawling mansion—and few can—you might be able to knock off some of its looks with just a few minor remodeling jobs.

With location already cemented, I drafted a list of interior and exterior "deal makers" first. Then I wrote up a list of items I preferred or hoped for in a home, but that were not necessary if I found something that included my deal makers. Here is what my list looked like:

DEAL MAKERS:

- Westside of Los Angeles
- Charming and quiet neighborhood, but near urban conveniences
- Two bedrooms or one plus loft/den (better for resale/roommate income)
- Well-maintained, cute complex
- Washer/dryer in the complex
- Light and breezy
- Spacious (enough to not feel claustrophobic)
- Turnkey, or needing few to no repairs or remodel
- Good closet space and storage
- Allows installation of hardwood floors
- Two full, or one and a half, bathrooms
- Price not to exceed my budgeted amount (based on my monthly mortgage projections)
- Low monthly HOA dues
- One parking space
- Safe area
- A fireplace or balcony or patio

MY NEGOTIABLES:

- Allows dogs
- Pool/Jacuzzi/sundeck
- Spacious layout
- Already has hardwood floors
- Washer/dryer in my unit, or the ability to hook them up
- Satellite hookup capability
- Small complex

What I got: a turnkey, two-bedroom, two-bath condo in the center of safe and sunny Santa Monica, housed in a medium-size complex with curbside appeal. While the complex has laundry facilities, it has no other amenities. But it does have a large, run-down community patio with a lot of potential. I also got my deal-making balcony (in fact, I got two), but no fireplace and no dogs allowed. I also had to fork over $54,000 more than was my personal limit. But it was worth it.

THE 411

A "turnkey" property is a term that real estate professionals use generically to describe a home in move-in condition, needing few to no repairs or renovations. Word to the wise: "Turnkey" is used loosely, and the standards by which a property could be defined as turnkey are blurry and subjective. "Turnkey" to some realtors could mean newly constructed, a home that they'd sell based on plans alone, before ground has even been broken. Meanwhile, other realtors might define a property as turnkey because it has all the bells and whistles of crown molding, freshly painted rooms, and granite countertops, but is not a new property. The term implies that all that's left to do, so to speak, is turn the keys over to the buyer.

Fortunately, I got most of what I'd set out for, but not all. The key to my success was twofold: compromise and seeing the condo's potential. I compromised on having a fireplace, but I got two balconies. I didn't want a complete "fixer-upper," even if I had to pay a little more (I knew I wouldn't have the time, energy, or financial resources to allocate to remodeling). I wanted a dog, but it was more important to me to move into a place that was open, bright, and airy. I wanted a Jacuzzi or a sundeck. Instead, I got a share of land that can, if my association members agree, be developed to hold either or both.

The other key to my success was walking into my would-be home and seeing its potential to become a sanctuary that reflected my personality and taste. My seller had decorated her home in a manner that minimized two components that were major selling points to me: its open, breezy layout and its exposure to sunlight.

I certainly don't have decorating or remodeling expertise, but I'd looked at enough properties to know I could take this blank canvas and paint a picture that suited my personal interior style. I did some preliminary pricing of how much energy and time it might cost me to do that. And before long, I was transforming the 966-square-foot box into my own charming palace. I achieved my dream simply by redecorating the space with minimal, light-colored furniture, adding decorative light switch covers, and personalizing it with farmers market vintage finds, like metal milk crates turned artsy kitchen cabinetry for displaying cookbooks, a cookie jar, and bottles of wine.

I had to accept a few drawbacks. First, the condo is an inner unit. So while I was on the top floor and saw pure blue sky when I looked out my windows, I also saw concrete, and into the windows of the other units that surrounded mine. That, of course, meant they could see into mine, too, with relative ease if my curtains were not closed.

Another drawback was that my unit was located next to the elevator, which, of course, was the main artery that allowed my neighbors to enter and exit their own homes. In addition, while I was drawn to the open, bright appeal of the condo, created in large part by the large sliding glass doors that serve as walls on either side of my unit, what draws you to a place can also end up being the same trait that annoys you. Hence, I pondered whether these doors that opened onto a publicly accessible balcony would ultimately become an invasion of my privacy. (While I'm gregarious by nature, being friendly when I'm not in the mood is exhausting. There are just some days when I want to create a makeshift cave and not see or talk to a single person.)

And then there was the most considerable drawback: the asking price. It was $76,000 over my intended limit. But when I did my initial walk-through, I knew I'd found a gem. Something in my gut told me not to worry about the price. It was close enough, and if it was meant to be, I could negotiate a more affordable amount. And that's just what I did.

I researched with my accountant and loan officer to see what I could comfortably afford and be approved for before beginning the negotiating process. In the end, I spent only $54,000 over my limit. The property was worth it to me. Besides, once you've decided to take the plunge into such hefty debt, shrugging off another $54,000 seemed like no sweat.

Have you determined your own home's deal makers and negotiables? Use my list to help you begin. Add to it your own heart's

desires regarding interior and exterior, but be sure to place them
under the appropriate heading. Chances are, you may end up in
your home longer than you'd originally anticipated, and you don't
want to underestimate what you really require to be happy.

TOP TEN ITEMS TO CONSIDER

1. What are your remodeling limitations: roofing, electrical,
   plumbing, structural, painting, new cabinetry, flooring?

2. How many neighbors do you want, and how close do you
   want them to be?

3. How much land do you want or need?

4. What kind of landscaping resources and needs are you
   willing to take on?

5. Are natural-disaster insurance and other benefits for
   the complex covered in your homeowners' association
   (HOA) fees?

6. Do any registered sex offenders live in the area?

7. How secure is your building?

8. Who are your neighbors? Do you want to live in an area or
   a complex that has children or allows pets?

9. Is an ecofriendly home with energy-saving features,
   recycling bins, and solar panels important to you?

10. What type of parking is suitable for you? Do you require a
    garage, or is a partially covered carport sufficient? Might you
    require a more secured, underground spot? And is guest
    parking a priority for you? You might also consider available
    street parking spaces, and rules and regulations that you'll
    be fined for violating.

CREATE YOUR OWN HOME PERSONAL AD

DEAL MAKERS: _____

_____

_____

_____

_____

_____

_____

_____

_____

NEGOTIABLES: _____

_____

_____

_____

_____

_____

_____

_____

_____

eight

Safety and the Single Woman

I have a recurring nightmare in which a faceless stranger is about to attack me. And just as I open my mouth wide to scream, nothing, not even the faintest sound, comes out. Silence strikes in the moment of fear. And I instantly awaken, sweating profusely.

Whether you're like me, struck by the occasional safety-related nightmare, or not, the single most important factor in buying a home as a single woman is not location for resale value, size, or even closet space. Your top priority is your personal safety. Period.

I didn't choose to house hunt on the Westside of Los Angeles solely because its easygoing beach community fit my personality best. Because the Westside is known for its low crime rate, it felt like a natural choice, a place where I could live and feel safe

walking around with minimal concern about lurking danger—
as long as I'm aware of my surroundings as I go about my day.

DO YOUR RESEARCH

Before you buy, check out your potential neighborhood for registered sex offenders. The federal government instituted Megan's
Law in 1996, which incorporates two measures to ensure your
safety. One component of Megan's Law requires convicted sex
offenders to register their current addresses with authorities.
The other component involves community notification: Federal
law mandates that every state develop a procedure for notifying
residents of sex offenders residing in their area. Each state differs in how it reports the information, as well as in its provisions
about sex-offender registration. Contact your local law enforce-
ment agency or inquire with your city administration to find out
how you can determine whether registered sex offenders (or how
many) live in the area you're considering buying in. Check out
your state's laws and more resources at www.sexcriminals.com.
Keep in mind, however, that convicted sex offenders don't always
register as they're required to. Also note that sex-offender information is free from your local authorities—so be wary of websites
that request payment.

Buying a property in a low-crime area was a good start, but
it was certainly not the only safety measure I employed upon em-
barking on my search for the perfect condo. No way. Potential
predators exist in even the safest areas. Small town, suburbia, or

big city, disturbed people come in all different sizes and races, and they're not only men.

When I purchased my humble abode in Santa Monica, California, I went into it knowing that I was also buying peace of mind—that my property value wasn't likely to decrease, and that my personal safety would be highly protected. Most of the crimes that happen in the city are petty thefts—so petty, in fact, that the police have little to do but set up jaywalking and traffic violation stings. I should know—I've been busted for both.

With my new investment situated atop a three-story building with security gates and cameras—and in the center of the complex safely surrounded by nothing but my new neighbors—I do feel blanketed with a sense of security. When I first bought my home, I walked with an air of relaxation, even leaving my sliding glass doors open and front door ajar while I ran down to the mailbox or the laundry room. *My neighbors are proud homeowners, too, I thought, a community of people who respect their homes and their neighbors.* And then one night, everything changed. My recurring nightmare turned into a near reality and forced me to reconsider my sense of security.

I had been living in my new condo for nearly three months. I delighted in acting like Little Miss Debbie Decorator, and proudly displayed my home to my friendly neighbors, who'd stop by to check things out.

It felt like *Melrose Place*. I'd never had that sense of community in any of the rental homes I'd lived in before. There were the outgoing female subletters about my age who lived just down the hall, one of whom I instantly bonded with; we decided we were kindred spirits. And there were Hazel and Gertrude, two elderly ladies who lived beside each other and just across the hall from me. Hazel was meek, but nice as could be. Gertrude was a spry, happy-go-lucky woman who had a weekly gentleman caller and a midafternoon hot toddy every day. I took to Gertrude instantly. She recounted her love affairs in more vivid detail than any romance novel could.

Also living in the building were several other young, professional married couples, each with their own interesting dynamics, as well as two attractive, nice thirtysomething guys who lived side by side.

And then there was Tom, the fiftysomething, gregarious, redheaded Irishman whom I'd occasionally run into as I entered and exited the building. He was a jovial guy, a Santa Claus of sorts. We exchanged pleasantries in our brief encounters. He'd inquire about my work or workouts. I'd engage just enough to be polite. It was innocent enough, or so I thought.

Late one quiet evening, I was writing in my new living room. My curtains were drawn, and only the faint background noise from my TV was audible. I started getting sleepy, and I decided to retire for the evening.

I shut off the TV and all the lights and proceeded toward my brightly lit bedroom. I stepped into my room and nearly shouted out in shock at what I saw standing before me: a silhouette of a man standing on my bedroom balcony, with his face and hands pressed firmly against my screen door as he peered through the sheers. As in my nightmare, I opened my mouth to scream, but nothing but a faint gasp escaped. I was immobilized by fear.

Upon hearing my gasp, the unwanted visitor calmly said, "Oh, don't be afraid." I recognized the Irish accent instantly. I let my guard down a little, and without thinking, I stupidly walked toward the unlocked screen door. "What's going on, Tom?" I asked nervously.

Tom started chatting me up, as if his being on my balcony and gazing into my bedroom were normal and justified, not totally unusual and creepy. An occasional slur of his words tipped me off to the fact that he'd been drinking. And despite how weirded out it made me feel, I pushed my instincts aside and talked myself out of thinking he shouldn't be there.

Without thinking clearly, I sprang into action. In a feeble attempt to quickly get my own Peeping Tom off my balcony and away from my home, I opened the screen door and calmly engaged in superficial conversation with the perpetrator. Luckily, Tom grew tired and left peacefully within a few minutes.

My heart racing, I darted back into my bedroom, closed the sliding glass door, and locked it behind me as fast as I could. I felt completely violated. The sense of safety I had allowed to insulate me from the dangers of living alone had been shattered. I pulled the curtains shut and curled up in bed in the fetal position, bawling as it hit me hard how threatened and vulnerable I felt. I yelled into the silent air in anger—at my Peeping Tom for violating my safe haven, and at myself for foolishly putting the violator's feelings before my own so he didn't feel awkward. I yelled at God, blaming my own fate and the fact that I didn't have a partner or a friend there to protect me, comfort me, and ensure my safety.

THE 411

Listen to your instincts! If you get even a whisper that your life might be in danger, don't disregard your inner suspicions because you're afraid of being embarrassed about misinterpreting signals or don't want to hurt someone else's feelings. Such hesitation minimizes your self-worth and could cost you your life. In addition, don't take matters into your own hands. Call 911 immediately and proclaim, "I'm in imminent danger"—and whenever possible, use a landline. Often, in larger cities, an emergency call made from a cellular phone is automatically transferred to a centralized dispatch system. As a result, your call has to be transferred to your local area code before you can have a response team en route to attend to your needs. Those extra three to ten minutes could determine your fate.

The next day, I told a few neighbors I'd befriended about my experience. One of the thirtysomething single guys down the hall took it upon himself to be on the lookout for Tom, and to confront him on my behalf. Meanwhile, my fun female neighbor and her boyfriend made sure the perpetrator saw us and overheard our conversation about the incident.

Insomnia ensued for a total of three months following the incident. Only after taking some important, and perhaps overdue, safety precautions was I able to eventually overcome my insecurities and sleep peacefully again. My first-time homebuying naiveté had been stolen from me. I decided to take my safety into my own hands.

TWENTY-FIVE TIPS FOR PROTECTING YOURSELF IN YOUR OWN HOME

1. If possible, do not buy a unit on the ground floor.

2. Buy a home with secured parking.

3. Change your locks upon moving into a new place, and get a deadbolt if possible.

4. Make sure locks on your windows and sliding glass doors function properly.

5. Lock your windows and doors while you're out and while you're home.

6. Invest in adjustable window stops. They allow windows to be open, but not wide enough for an outside intruder to get in.

7. Reinforce windows and sliding glass doors by wedging a broom or a piece of wood in their tracks, making them difficult to move.

8. Mix up your daily routine.

9. Get a dog.

10. Create a neighborhood watch group, join your homeowners' association, or build a friendship with a trusted neighbor. Consider giving him or her a key in case of emergencies.

11. Pull your curtains closed at night to make it difficult for outsiders to see in.

12. Keep valuables out of view of the windows.

13. Invest in a home alarm system.

14. Make sure all entrances and walkways are well lit.

15. Condo and co-op owners: Police your complex for secured common areas with public access; monitor street access to a fire escape.

16. Trim any unmanicured bushes or trees that make reaching your windows easy.

17. Make sure garage units, attached or separate, are also secured.

18. Make a pact with a close friend or family member about calling to check in on a night you're returning home alone.

19. Don't give out seemingly innocuous but personal information to people you don't know well. Information as simple as interests, travel plans, marital status, and work routine can all be used to target you as a victim.

20. Keep your whereabouts a secret. Don't let mail or newspapers stack up; ask a friend to pick it up for you. Invest in light timers to turn on automatically while you're away. And don't leave drapes and shades closed.

21. Install a peephole in your front door and ask visitors to identify themselves before letting them in.

22. List only your last name and first initial in phone directories and on mailboxes.

23. If you come home and find a door or window open or any signs of forced entry, don't go in. Go to the nearest phone and call the police.

24. Don't give information about yourself to strangers over the phone, or admit that you are alone.

25. If you have an answering machine, do not give out any personal information or say, "I'm not home" on the message.

I think the most traumatizing part of my whole ordeal was knowing I'd willingly engaged in conversation with my would-be perpetrator. Tom had used his familiarity and my living situation to take advantage of me. I was angry at him, but even more so at myself for not catching on to his game earlier; I'd always prided myself on being observant and good at reading people and their intentions, after all.

Since that night, I've had to learn to not be so trusting with people just because they're familiar faces. Without sacrificing my naturally gregarious disposition, I'm much more conscious of whom I give personal information to, no matter how seemingly harmless it is. And I make every effort to be present in the moment and take note of my gut's notions. Just as I had learned to do in my romantic relationships and friendships, I would have to learn slowly to trust and respect my neighbors, and only when they respected me first.

About six months later, I was faced with yet another frightening and potentially dangerous situation in my new home. Only this time, I listened to my instincts and was proactive.

My building was undergoing some major construction right outside my unit. So not only were I and my home visible every day to the six or so twentysomething construction workers, but also, as president of my homeowners' association, I had to interact with them on occasion. I was in a position of authority and would need to oversee their work and answer their questions.

Over the first couple of weeks, I was my typical take-charge but considerate self. I even baked chocolate chip cookies and gave them to the guys to show our appreciation for their hard work. We developed a professional rapport, and I was not thrown by their stopping me in the hallway, needing guidance regarding their responsibilities, as I set off for work in the mornings.

Although I hadn't felt uncomfortable in those weeks working with the guys, they were obviously young and somewhat inexperienced in appropriate professional behavior. One worker in particular seemed to take a bit of a liking to me—I sensed it because of the way he looked at me, and because he needed to talk to me more frequently, often away from the other guys—but he hadn't done or said anything to me that made me concerned.

Then one morning, as I was in my bedroom, getting dressed for work, I was startled by a knock on my front door. I wasn't accustomed to morning visitors. I opened the door to find the young construction worker who I sensed was crushing on me standing there. We stood in my doorway as he explained that he needed guidance on some work that someone else on the board had asked him to complete, a request I hadn't known anything about. A whisper blew gently up my back. This time, I paid attention to it.

As our brief conversation ended, the worker said, "You look great, by the way. And wow, look at your home! Do you live here all alone?" I quickly shooed him away from my front door, locking it swiftly behind me.

In a matter of minutes, I was taken back to that day when my Peeping Tom violated my safety. And when I arrived at my office that morning, I immediately sprang into action. I sent an email to my thirtysomething male neighbor who had befriended me (I secretly called him Hot Neighbor), explaining the incident and asking him to have lunch with me in my home one afternoon while the workers were there. He agreed.

Needless to say, I never had a problem with that worker again. Meanwhile, I continue to sleep comfortably at night knowing Hot Neighbor has my back and is only a quick call or knock away in case of an intruder, fire, or earthquake.

That leads me to the other kind of emergencies you need to be prepared for: fires and natural disasters. Whether you purchase a freestanding single-family home or move into a shared-living community, make sure to develop good habits and resources to protect yourself and your family in case disaster strikes. Below are some other disaster-preparedness suggestions that the National Crime Prevention Council (www.ncpc.org) offers.

PREPARATION IS YOUR BEST PROTECTION

1. Develop a communications plan for your family. Choose someone who does not live with you (preferably an out-of-town relative or friend) whom you and other family members can contact. Carry that person's contact information in your purse or wallet.

2. Memorize the out-of-town contact person's phone number. You may not have access to your cell phone where it's programmed.

3. Make sure children know the last name, phone number, and address for the out-of-town contact person.

4. Make sure every member of your family knows an alternate route home.

5. If family members can't get home, designate a meeting place.

6. Know your community's emergency evacuation route.

7. Learn how to shut off utilities, such as gas, electricity, and water—for both your home and your complex if you buy a condo or co-op.

8. Assemble an emergency-preparedness kit that will allow your family to camp out for three days. Assume you'll be without electricity and running water.

9. Store your emergency supplies in sealed containers, such as plastic tubs, taped shut.

10. Keep cash on hand; automated teller machines won't be working if the power is out.

11. Learn CPR and first aid to help with medical emergencies.

12. Learn about emergency plans for your children's school or daycare center.

13. Work with your neighborhood watch or civic association to create a disaster-preparedness plan.

nine

D o you remember your first job? I mean *real* job. Not just babysitting the neighbor kids for a few hours each week while their mom and dad were rocking their occasional big night out. I mean the first time you hit the pavement—probably around age fifteen to eighteen—feeling all dorky inside but probably a little excited, too, to ask complete strangers whether they were hiring.

I don't know about you, but I remember feeling mostly awkward and vulnerable. True, I camouflaged it well under my fancy-schmancy button-down top, slacks, and oh-so-trendy pumps. But not even my big-girl clothes could make me feel confident inside. Sure, outwardly I looked like I had it pulled together. But inside, I felt like people were looking at me as if I had a big pimple in the middle of my forehead and wasn't good enough to work in *their* store. Who did I think I was?

Homebuying for the first time is like any first, whether it's a first job or a first love: The experience is all new to you. New experiences can leave you feeling off-balance and fearful of the unknown, so it is important for you to gather as many facts as possible about what you're looking for *before* you buy. In the same way that dating a variety of people helps you recognize a good catch when you see one, knowing what you want in a home helps you weed out the things that simply aren't going to match your personality or needs.

One of the biggest things we need to do to prepare ourselves for employment, dating, and homeowning alike is make ourselves attractive and viable candidates. You are your most valuable asset, after all, and if your total package—your assets, appearance, and reputation—is an appealing one, it can make all the difference in whether you're taken seriously as a prospective buyer.

How do you get started? First, become prequalified. What is prequalification and how do you get it? In Chapter 10, I'll describe how, upon selecting my real estate agent, I immediately contacted a mortgage broker to help me feel more confident about the price range I could comfortably afford. Unbeknownst to me at the time, I was not only finding a suitable dollar amount for myself, but I was also informing my new "sales team" (real estate agent and mortgage broker). My financial situation empowered them to determine whether I was, in fact, a prospective homebuying candidate or just a single young woman with big aspirations but no financial backing. Despite the fact that women are often the breadwinners of their families, and that the number of single women buying homes has soared recently, it's important for single women to have everything worked out in advance. If you go in prepared, people won't have a chance to not take you seriously.

To first attract real estate market suitors, you need to build your most attractive financial package. Consider researching your prequalification for a loan prior to beginning your homebuying search. Doing so will set a realistic benchmark for you and your real estate agent regarding your price range. Assuming you'll need a loan, prequalification is like the resumé of a job candidate: If a potential employer likes what she reads on your resume, she'll bring you in for an interview, right? Same goes here.

THE 411

How does an institution decide how much money to loan you? It's based on a few personal financial factors that a bank or a mortgage broker will ask you. Some general prequalification questions include: What is your annual income? How much debt (overall) do you have? Do you have any additional sources of income? How long have you worked for your current employer?

A mortgage broker will take a financial "snapshot" of your monthly/annual financial outlook and help you determine what amount you might be able to afford for a mortgage payment. Your prequalifying figure will inform your sales team of your financial viability. It may also be just the house-hunting tool you need to answer your lingering questions regarding buying a home. Some of these questions may include: Can I afford the kind of house I want, and in the neighborhood I want to buy in at this time? Do I want to tie myself to a monthly mortgage of this amount just to buy where I want to, or should I consider spending less and buying elsewhere . . . which will leave me with more money to apply toward traveling, clothes, or decorating?

THE 411

Prequalifying for a loan is not a guarantee from a lender that you are preapproved for a loan. It is merely an educated guesstimate based on the information you provide for their consideration. It's in your best interest to be honest about your financial standing— both debt and earnings—to give yourself a true picture of what you can afford to buy and whether you can get a loan to back your purchase.

Once you know your prequalification status, you and your sales team can confidently begin your homebuying search. When your search yields a prospect or two that sufficiently matches your list of deal makers and negotiables (see Chapter 7), you'll want to secure a preapproval letter.

The preapproval letter is like the professional references you list on your resume, which can verify the accuracy of your resume and your reputation, just as a preapproval letter can stave off doubts about your viability as a homeowner.

Becoming preapproved for a loan means that one or more financial outlets have committed to you in writing that they will fund a loan on your behalf, up to a maximum specified amount, for buying a property. Securing a preapproval letter from a reputable financial institution is the most solid evidence you can offer a seller and her real estate agent that you can make good on your offer to buy her home (more on that in Chapter 12). This is especially important in a competitive market, and if you're faced with entering a bidding war for the home you hope to purchase.

 THE 411

Even if you're preapproved for a loan, a lender will not loan money to you if the home you want to buy doesn't meet the current market appraisal for it. In other words, if a seller is asking for a much higher price than what the official appraiser determines is the current market value for the home, a financial institution may not loan you the money to purchase it—even if you, the buyer, are willing to pay the money—for fear they won't be able to recoup their losses in resale if you default on the loan.

Before you receive a preapproval letter, financial institutions that are considering loaning you money will dig deep into your financial background. With your permission, they will review bank records, mutual fund and stock investments, and employment compensation documents. They will cross-reference outstanding debts—including credit cards and student and auto loans—to evaluate your history of making timely payments toward paying down your debt. If you have ever filed for bankruptcy or faced a foreclosure on a previous home, that information is sure to emerge in the preapproval process, and it may adversely affect whether a loan institution lends you money for your purchase.

One of the most valuable tools a loan institution utilizes in determining whether to loan you money is your credit report. They do this by reviewing your FICO scores (named after the company that developed the system—Fair Isaac Corporation). Think of FICO scores as being like the ACT, SAT, GRE, or GMAT scores that schools use as benchmark figures when considering potential students.

Unlike in academic test taking, though, you can get three different scores in homebuying. How? Each of the three reputable credit reporting companies—TransUnion (800-888-4213 or www.tuc.com), Experian (800-493-2392 or www.experian.com), and Equifax (800-685-1111 or www.equifax.com)—will individually review your credit history and give you a score based on their findings. Lenders then will likely calculate your average FICO score based on the scores that each of the three credit reporting companies provide to them—which can range from the 300s to the 900s. The higher you score on your FICO, the better. Generally speaking, a FICO score reaching into the high 700s or higher is regarded as super by a financial institution, and almost certainly guarantees you both a loan and a good mortgage rate.

THE 411

A lower FICO score typically ensures a higher interest rate on your mortgage payment. A lender will also likely require you to put more of your own money down up front, so that they reduce their risk by loaning you less money to purchase a place.

Even if your FICO score is respectable, lenders will usually demand clarification of any mark that suggests you might be a risky investment—and a multitude of items on your record could seem questionable.

When I was researching loans to buy my own home, a couple of items on my credit record raised red flags for potential lending institutions. First and foremost, I had absentmindedly forgotten to make a few credit card payments on time over the past couple of years, which lowered my score and caused concern for would-be lending companies because it raised the possibility that I might default on my mortgage payment. Second, they were suspicious of the secondary name on my checking account. I was bewildered that something this seemingly insignificant could raise eyebrows.

The second name on my checking account was my mother's. It had been there since I'd moved to California, more than twelve years earlier—when I was fresh out of college. I'd merely opened the account with her secondary signature because she had worked at the bank at the time, which created some cost-saving benefits for me. She'd long since changed jobs, but I never removed her from my account, in part out of sheer laziness, but mostly because I still got free checks. It was ironic that my innocuous $75-a-year savings scheme put my half-million-dollar loan at risk. Fortunately, because my mother's first name is my middle name, it was easy enough for my mortgage broker to explain away. Phew!

When my friend's mom, Ann (from Chapter 6), was applying for her first loan as a single homebuyer, she too dealt with a credit snafu. With a preapproval letter in hand, Ann was dismayed to learn that some lenders were questioning her credit report, not because of her income as a single mother, as she had feared, but rather because some official document in her credit history had erroneously listed her as a co-owner of the home she had previously lived in with her husband and children.

Talk about ironic. Because Ann's ex-husband had always overseen the family's money, Ann never even had an electric bill in her name, let alone on the title or deed of trust to their home. Ann's husband used his higher income as an excuse to control all his family's financial decisions, and ultimately to control Ann. His suffocating grip on her eventually grew into the greatest point of contention in their marriage. After they divorced, Ann's biggest concern was that she hadn't ever established credit for herself, since she'd married so young and had allowed everything to be credited in her husband's name.

So when Ann applied for a first-time homebuying loan (see Chapter 4) and was told she didn't qualify because she'd owned previously, she was enraged. The biggest obstacle in Ann's marriage was now becoming her biggest hurdle in buying her first home. Talk about frustrating! Ann never dreamed that her ex-husband would still be haunting her and affecting her financial well-being. Fortunately, her mortgage broker was able to get the mistake corrected on Ann's credit report, and Ann successfully got the loan and her first home.

So, what do you do if you have a questionable credit history, or if you discover an error on your credit report that is adversely affecting your credit score? Correct it. If there's an error on your report, federal law requires a credit reporting company to correct your record within thirty days of receiving proof of the inaccuracy. However, it is usually up to you to provide the proof to the agency, which can be a long and tedious process. But cleaning up your credit record is the most important thing you can do for yourself both for buying a home and for securing any other potential loan. The Federal Trade Commission can give you more information on how to correct an error. Request information online at www.ftc.gov or by phone at 877-382-4357.

TOP TWELVE FACTORS THAT COULD NEGATIVELY AFFECT YOUR CREDIT SCORE

1. Recent foreclosure on a home
2. Recent bankruptcy
3. Recent missed or late payments on loans, including credit card, auto, or school loans
4. A large sum of current loan debt
5. Large sums of available, unused debt (for instance, credit cards totaling large credit limits, even if you have little debt applied against them at that time)

6. No or very little credit history

7. Too many open or new credit accounts

8. Recent closing of credit cards or other forms of credit lines

9. Allowing too many lenders (more than one) to run your credit report within a fourteen-day period

10. Substantial high-interest credit debt (like credit cards), but little to no investment debt (like real estate, stocks, bonds, or mutual funds)

11. Financial debt from a spouse, child, friend, or family member for whom you have agreed to cosign your name on a loan of any sort

12. Being a recent identity-theft victim

Cleaning up a credit mess or establishing a credit history can be difficult and time consuming. The best way to deal with a credit mess is to set a new standard of financial excellence moving forward. You can start determining what shape your credit is in by requesting and reviewing your credit report annually. You are entitled to one free personal credit report in a twelve-month period. Visit www.annualcreditreport.com to make your request. Should an additional report become necessary within a twelve-month period, they are relatively inexpensive and worth the nominal fee to protect your financial reputation. You will be able to check inaccuracies, marks against your score, and what, if any, history you have established. Finding out what your record says may be scary. But you can't fix what you don't know exists.

JUMP-START YOUR CREDIT HISTORY TODAY

1. Get a checking or savings account with a debit/credit card in your name. If possible, get an account that offers over-draft protection (which covers your charges up to a pre-specified amount, even when you don't have enough money in your account to do so).

2. Use your debit/credit card to pay for your bills whenever you can.

3. Apply for a couple low-interest, no-annual-fee credit cards. Use them, but responsibly.

4. Put rental, car, and utility bills in your name and make payments on time.

5. Apply for a department store credit card and use it responsibly.

6. Get a financially responsible and trustworthy cosigner. After a year's worth of charging and making payments on time, apply to have their name removed from your account.

Okay, now that you know what it takes to get your financial package prepared to buy your own home, it's also important for you to get your appearance in check. Why? Because, let's face it, looks matter. I know—I witnessed people's biases firsthand.

I tackled the early days of home hunting simply by cruising through my neighborhood and stopping at numerous open houses. It was a great way to get my feet wet and see how the process looked from that vantage point. It also gave me a good indication of what I could get for my money.

I also visited homes that were unrepresented by an agent, an experience that allowed me to develop my own sense of taste and make my own judgments before getting a second opinion about a place I might like. Most of my house browsing took place on weekend afternoons, when the last thing I wanted to do was get dolled up after a full week of looking presentable for other people. But because you only get one shot at a first impression, I'd pull myself together in my smart casual attire: a nice pair of jeans, a stylish fitted top, and low heels. I looked more respectable and serious about my potential as a buyer. And it helped me mask my inner insecurity that I was completely winging this whole home-buying thing.

One Saturday afternoon, I decided I'd drop by a few open houses at nearby condominium complexes. As I was about to leave my apartment, I invited my roommate Claudia to come along. She wasn't doing anything particularly fancy that Saturday, and she was dressed in her comfy house clothes: faded jeans, oversize sweatshirt with a couple of small paint stains, flip-flops, and not a lick of makeup.

We breezed through a couple of homes before stumbling upon one I took interest in. I stopped to talk more with the selling agent. Claudia was at my side. She listened intently to the agent's answers to my questions, as she had also begun thinking about investing in a home soon. Claudia even asked a few questions of her own, and they were good ones. After all, she's a smart young woman with a high-paying corporate job, despite the fact that her appearance that day suggested otherwise.

That's why I was shocked by the way the selling agent (another woman, mind you) dismissed her completely. The agent looked me in the eyes when responding to Claudia's questions.

It was as if she were saying Claudia wasn't worth wasting her energy on. I was so offended on my friend's behalf that we left immediately.

But that experience did teach me a good lesson. As much as I'd like to believe otherwise, people make gross generalizations and judgments based on appearances. That particular agent assumed Claudia couldn't have afforded to buy and dismissed her. Being presentable and pulled together in preparation for homebuying is, as it turns out, as important as turning up for a job interview in appropriate attire. You never know when you're going to run into the perfect home, so it's better to be prepared.

Looking sharp and together is also important upon meeting your agent for the first time. While appearances certainly can't dictate the size of a person's bank account or debt, they can certainly convey someone's seriousness about homebuying. And considering that an agent's income is dependent upon their client list, a smart agent may weigh your overall appearance as a factor in deciding whether to take you on, or how much effort they'll put into your search. If you're not serious about your search, why should they be? And, not surprisingly, when it comes time to meet with bank officers and mortgage brokers—people whom you are asking to entrust their money to you—a well-groomed hairstyle and buttoned-up attire will serve as your allies in securing the money you need.

Shaping up your financials, credit report, and appearance are critical before you start house hunting. Homebuying, while personal to you, is a business transaction to others. As a smart, savvy, independent woman, treat homebuying with the same

diligence with which you conquer your career. Proper preparation
will bring you that much closer to success.

ten

Your Quest for the Right Real Estate Agent

F inding a good partner in life is no easy task. But then, that's the most obvious statement ever. You want to find a person who really gets you, supports you, attends to your needs. Finding the right match in a real estate agent carries the same importance in terms of finding a home that suits you. This person is your front man or woman. When hiring a real estate agent or broker (a broker and an agent act similarly but differ in accreditation), you want someone who serves and protects your interest, as well as someone who represents you favorably in both searching for your home and negotiating its purchase.

You'll recall from earlier chapters that I originally began my house hunt with an independent real estate agent whom I met randomly by wandering into an open house in the neighborhood I was renting in at the time. David was an affable guy, and was gracious enough to take a little time with me during my walk-through of the property to explain a bit about the whole real estate process. I especially appreciated it because, characteristically, I jumped right into the idea of homebuying without following a guide or reading any materials about how it all worked first. During that initial meeting, David agreed to take me on as a client. I felt lucky at the time that he was willing to work with such a newbie.

DEMYSTIFY YOUR "007"

There are three types of buyer's agents:

1. Buyer's agent: Works only for the buyer and receives her commission when the buyer purchases a property. (The only catch is that a buyer's agent's commission depends on the property's purchase price, requiring you to be even more knowledgeable about a potential home's market value.)

2. Seller's agent: Works strictly for the seller and receives her commission from the sale of the home. (The selling agent's paycheck is also dependent on the sale price of the home, creating an inherent conflict as well.)

3. Dual agent: Acts as an agent for both the seller and the buyer. (While this type of buy-sell risks conflict, it may yield a savings in the commission percentage you pay out at the sale, and is worth considering.)

My first mistake was not doing my research. I can't say I ended up with any awful stories to recount here, but I can say fairly certainly that minimal research (like what you're smartly doing just by reading this book) could have saved me a lot of time.

My second mistake was being grateful to David for taking me on as a client. This wasn't because David wasn't a kind person; it was because, in the end, real estate agents make their money from your purchase—a commission typically ranging from 3 to 7 percent, which comes out of the seller's pocket (or, frankly, yours). This is the first thing you should realize: A real estate agent needs you in order to make money. This important awareness will empower you to be more selective in whom you choose as your real estate agent or broker, and how you select her. Remember that she is a reflection of you, and choose wisely.

THE 411

California-licensed real estate expert Justin Rubin explains, "Real estate agents with new homes to sell will often hold 'price opinions' or 'sneak previews.' In the real estate world, a selling agent will hold these nonpublic events with other realtors to bounce ideas off about pricing the property. And many times in that price-opinion meeting, the realtors will tell their clients about this property about to hit the market. This also serves the selling agent in driving foot traffic to the public 'open house.'"

David was a part-time real estate agent and a full-time, self-employed accountant. He lived in the Valley, just over the hill from the Westside, where I'd determined I wanted to purchase my home. He would generally make the half-hour trek to the

Westside once or twice during the week in the beginning of our partnership. On weekends, we'd team up and caravan from open house to open house, ones we'd established beforehand I'd be interested in.

David showed me a lot of properties in the nearly two years I was with him. We went through two home negotiations together. I lost out on both: The first time was because of my first-time homebuying pride at bidding time. The second time was because of David's downfalls as a realtor.

No one's perfect. And in a relationship, you have to be willing to overlook someone's little flaws if you're going to have a harmonious and blissful union . . . or so I'm told. While I'm still learning to navigate the dating world, I do know from experience that I'm an excellent businesswoman. I'm certainly not the shrewdest or the smartest, but I'm good at it and don't settle for mediocre work, especially not when I'm paying for good service. And when you're investing in a real estate agent, that is exactly what you're doing. Just because the money isn't exchanged up front doesn't mean you should expect less service and quality. In fact, everything leading up to a sale is what should tell you whether you've got a good partner in your agent. That's her moment to show you what she's made of. Why? Because you owe her nothing and can switch agents at any time—unless you've signed a contract (which I strongly urge you not to do!).

Inexperienced in homebuying as I was, I stuck with David and he stuck with me. In the beginning, he was quite gung ho, and would always meet me whenever I wanted to see a place. But as time wore on, he'd often send me to look at them on my own.

And there were a lot of homes. In one regard, looking on my own was good, because I saw a lot of what was out there, and that helped me gauge what I could get for my money. Moreover, I learned what I wasn't willing to settle for with the amount I had to spend.

Also positive was the fact that I became acutely aware that David wasn't a part of the Westside real estate community. He wasn't in the loop with other Westside realtors. This meant he had limited resources for learning about new properties that were about to be put on the market. Nor did he have the inside scoop on whether a place I was interested in had another offer out already. These inadequacies greatly affected that second home I bid on and lost.

It was a charming town home in Brentwood, California, a small, upscale community of families and young professionals that was notorious for being the neighborhood where O. J. Simpson lived before and during his murder trial. The town home I was looking at had hardwood floors and a washer and dryer in the unit, and its walls were painted a subdued yellow that I loved. It was exactly what I was looking for, and the biggest bonus was that the price was in my range. And though it seemed a bit low, I knew I wanted to make an offer right away.

THE 411

Sometimes a real estate agent will purposely list a property at a price lower than market value to encourage a buying frenzy. This practice typically garners numerous bids, ultimately driving the final sale price substantially higher than the asking price, and often to more than what the seller had expected to sell the place for.

I consulted with David about what I should offer. I'd already lost out on the first property I'd bid on, and I didn't want to chance losing this one, too. Considering it was a true sellers' market at the time (meaning that home sales were high and inventory was low), David suggested offering the asking price. Trusting his professional experience, that's just what I did.

David sent in the offer. Three days and several phone calls later, the selling agent finally returned David's call. The seller had accepted another offer. David discovered, only after the fact, that there had been multiple offers on the home, and that my bid of the asking price was one of the lower bids. He was upset that the selling agent hadn't informed us so that I could have had the option of placing a higher counteroffer. And I was frustrated that David didn't have better relationships with the realtors in the area, who could have told him about the competing bids before I made my offer. I learned the hard way that sometimes you get only one shot, so you'd better make it count.

THE 411

In an average housing market, there is a relatively equal balance of supply and demand, meaning homes for sale versus homes sold. Oftentimes, however, conditions for buying a home favor either the seller or the buyer.

A "buyer's market" exists when there's an increase in new homes being put up for sale while a sizeable number of homes are already up for sale. This environment results in home prices decreasing, making the market prime and affordable.

A "seller's market" exists when the number of homes already up for sale is on the lean side and new homes for sale are few and far between. This environment causes home prices to surge, and often results in multiple offers.

Another of David's downfalls (or mine, as it were) was that I ignored the little voice in my head telling me that David was just waiting for the right opportunity to hit on me. He'd alluded to hanging out outside of our property searches, offering to take me surfing with his daughter sometime. He'd occasionally and nonchalantly inquire about my boyfriend status. I dodged his invitations each time, but it started grating on my nerves when seeing him felt like a chore. But my loyalty bone is thick, and, just as I'd feel about a hairdresser whom I'd outgrown but had employed for a long time, I didn't have the heart to betray David.

But then one day, when David and I had arranged to meet for lunch to review listings, he called ten minutes beforehand to cancel. He said he was stuck in a meeting with one of his accounting clients. Only then did I finally allow myself to walk away from him. This was business, after all, and I realized where I was on his food chain. I needed a realtor who made me a priority. I seized the opportunity to make a clean, guilt-free break from David.

After that was when I decided to drop my search for an entire year to travel and save money for a down payment. When I decided to start back up again, I found my new realtor, Justin, through a referral—from an acquaintance at work, who'd recently purchased her condominium on the Westside of town, where I wanted to buy.

My initial meeting with Justin took place at his Sotheby's office in Brentwood. While I was impressed that a recognizable and revered real estate brand backed him, I was also intimidated. The offices were located in an affluent business complex. Upon entering, I was greeted by a nice, conservatively dressed woman, who answered phones in a sleek-looking receptionist area. I waited in one of several plush seats lined up against the eggshell-white walls. Boy, was I glad I'd decided to don my professional attire for this particular meeting.

The receptionist rang for Justin. I sat quietly in the lobby, looking at numerous awards and certificates in expensive-looking frames displayed proudly on the wall behind her. *Who am I kidding?* I thought. *I can't afford a realtor from here.*

Just as I contemplated running out before I had a chance to be embarrassed, Justin came out from around the corner, wearing an endearing smile, and gave me a firm handshake. He seemed to have a friendly, outgoing disposition and—although I know looks can be deceiving, especially among salespeople—an honest look about him. He was handsomely dressed in a suit and tie. He ushered me into a nearby conference room—sizable, filled with several black leather chairs and a big flat-screen television.

Justin and I took the first twenty minutes getting to know each other, exchanging pleasantries about our shared acquaintance, what kind of home I was looking for, and whether I'd been searching long. I summarized my house-hunting experience the first time around. I was clear on what I wanted in a home (see Chapter 7) and the price range I thought was affordable. And then, feeling out of my league, I cringed and said, "Justin, I don't think I can afford you."

With a gentle voice and a kind smile, Justin put me at ease: "You'd be surprised." He reassured me that while what I wanted for the amount I was willing to pay was going to be tough to discover in such a sellers' market, he felt confident that it was reasonable and that we'd find it. Justin supported his credibility in the real estate community by touting his success with home sales and purchases in the area, and his strong relationships in the Westside community. He also told me something I didn't appreciate fully at the time, but that now seems fairly important in selecting a real estate agent: He had gone through the process twice himself.

LIKE A VIRGIN

While a newly licensed real estate agent or broker can be just as capable, savvy, and professional as—and perhaps even hungrier than—more established ones, you'll want to know how many scenarios she's experienced that will help her negotiate and navigate you through a successful transaction. If a realtor is inexperienced, but you like and trust her, make sure she's backed by a reputable brokerage and surrounded by professionals who can guide her. A good real estate agent, whether virgin or veteran, will still brainstorm with colleagues and management teams on various issues, properties, and clients.

Justin was professional, smart, and assertive. It was easy to see he was a man who liked a challenge, and yet he was plenty affable. And I liked that about him. But it also concerned me. Why? Well, although this is business, you can't help but develop personal kinships with people, much like I had with David initially. I was worried that Justin might become frustrated with me after a certain amount of time if I didn't find a property I liked. I am a woman who knows what she wants, after all, and I'm not willing to settle for less . . . especially when I'm paying for it. And so, out of fairness, and mainly to protect myself from feeling guilt-ridden later on in our relationship, like I'd begun to feel with David, I said to Justin, "I am motivated to buy, but only if it's the right fit for me. And I don't know how long it might take. I'm afraid you'll be upset with me if it doesn't happen right away."

His reply was equal parts honest and comforting: "Jennifer, I don't care how long it takes. I'm in no rush. My job is to find you a home that makes you happy. I will not be upset with you if that takes a year or more." And with that understanding, we forged an instant mutual respect for each other and became a team.

From there, in that same first meeting, Justin and I talked next steps. For me, it was getting my credit score (see Chapter 9). Next, we finalized a reasonable price range. And even though I thought I had a good idea of what I could afford to buy in a home, I needed help in determining a comfortable, final monthly mortgage cost before I could commit to house shopping with Justin, as others had warned me that a plethora of hidden charges were associated with homebuying and could increase my monthly mortgage payment.

Justin offered a handful of mortgage brokers for me to contact. I recognized one name from the same acquaintance who'd referred me to Justin, and Justin offered to dial him up on the spot. Right then and there, I knew I'd found my Mr. Right—of realtors, that is.

Justin, I was quickly learning, was expedient and a one-stop-shopping real estate machine. And that was just what I needed in my life—someone who could take control so I could relax a bit until decision-making time came.

YOUR REAL ESTATE AGENT LITTLE BLACK BOOK

1. Is she licensed by the state you're buying in, and is her license current?

2. Is he knowledgeable in the specific areas you want to buy in—the current market landscape for the type of home you're looking to purchase, the safety of the area, and potential city zoning plans?

3. Does she have strong industry relationships in the area you want to buy in, with other real estate agents, property inspectors, mortgage brokers, escrow companies, and the like?

4. Is he a strong negotiator who commands attention when he speaks?

5. Does she listen carefully to what is important to you in a home, and to your concerns?

6. Does he actively research properties for you to see based on your specifications, and does he follow through?

7. Does she, not her assistant, accompany you during most or all walk-throughs?

8. Does he pressure you to buy a home, or to spend more money than feels comfortable for you?

9. Does she communicate with you in a way that works for you? Does she speak to you in laymen's terms? Does she take the time to educate you on the process? Or does she act condescending and make you feel stupid for asking questions or disagreeing with her perspective on a topic?

10. Does he make you feel safe, and not mix too much pleasure with business?

11. Does she offer up her recent activity list? (And if she doesn't, request it.) On it, note her success with properties similar to what you're looking to buy.

12. Does he offer references from recent happy homeowners he's represented? (And if he doesn't, request their contact information.) Then be sure to check.

13. Has she purchased her own home in the past? While it's not a deal maker, will that knowledge help her to better understand your perspective as a new homeowner?

14. Does he have a BlackBerry, Treo, or iPhone to use for interacting with you quickly? In a busy world, instant emails and texts have become the way many new potential homebuyers prefer to communicate. And in real estate, because time is often of the essence, and with today's technological advances, there's no reason you shouldn't feel like a priority.

Justin wasted no time. He and I started our search that very weekend. He'd email me a list of properties we'd caravan to. Justin was there by my side through every one, making a mental note of my comments. They all fit my location, two-bedroom/two-bath specifications, and price-range needs. But Justin paid attention to the details, too. He noted what I liked and, more important, what I didn't like for each one, such as no open layout or natural light, an unkempt exterior, a too-small unit, a too-big complex, and too much remodeling required.

On day three of my search, Justin proactively emailed and phoned me about homes he thought I should check out. We made a list for the week based on my preferences and availability. He took charge of scheduling the appointments with individual selling agents, and I didn't have to lift a finger.

On day four, I was pleasantly surprised when Justin called in the morning to offer to swing by my office and pick me up to start our laundry list of the day's appointments. You mean I didn't have to navigate, look at the places by myself, be in charge of figuring out where each of the places were, and then get back to him about the ones I liked? Sign me up, please!

Together, my realtor and I tore through four homes in a couple of hours. I saw some that seemed close, but not close enough. Between appointments, Justin and I bonded, sharing a few laughs and stories.

Days five, six, seven, and eight were more of the same. Bonnie and Clyde were on an aggressive path. Justin was proving to be tireless and motivated. He made house hunting seem more like an adventure and less like something else to add to my to-do list. He listened to my complaints about each place, and he talked me through my questions: "How much do you think it would cost me to put in hardwood floors?" "Would the homeowners' association let me install a skylight?" "Do you think the resale value for this particular property will do well?" and so on.

Day nine, we rested.

And on day ten, lightning struck. We'd found a charming home just around the corner from my work that I liked, and that had already been on the market for thirty days. It didn't exactly match what I'd hoped for in a first home: there was no pool or fireplace, and the complex was larger than I preferred. But I'd seen enough homes to know it offered more of what I wanted than most, and it was in a price range I might be able to afford. It had potential.

Not wanting to show my cards, I didn't convey my interest too much during the tour. But as soon my partner in crime and I made our getaway, we hashed it out. I listed the pros and the cons of the property. Justin served as my sounding board. He did not try to sway me one way or the other. We discussed market value, and whether Justin felt confident that I could negotiate a lower price for the property.

He advised me not to make a decision that day. I was in no rush; it was only day ten of my new search. Still, I left thinking, *It can't be this easy!*

I sat with my thoughts for a couple of days. I talked with friends about my find. I also ran some figures by my mortgage broker, based on my top buying price for this particular property. Meanwhile, my house matchmaker continued gathering other prospects for me to consider. He also stayed in contact with the selling realtor, determining if there were any other offers on the table and whether she was holding any upcoming open houses for the unit. (An open house would obviously draw attention to the property and garner potential competing bids.)

The realtor was, in fact, holding an open house that very weekend, which would give me an opportunity to look at it again. This time, I wanted to bring along my friend and potential roommate. I rolled the dice and decided to let fate lead me. My friend's opinion was reassuring, but she did not try to influence me in either direction. It was ultimately my decision, a choice I'd be committing to living with for some time to come. I decided I needed one more "date" with my trusty realtor to resolve a couple of issues percolating inside me.

Justin patiently arranged for another private walk-through just a couple of days later. He pointed out a few details that he thought were uncommon finds: hardwood floors in a top unit, the chandelier, crown molding. But he also left me on my own to feel the space and ponder my thoughts. He'd been very perceptive and picked up on my style early on: He knew to educate me and offer opinions, but not pressure me one way or the other. Justin's approach was probably his greatest strength as a realtor.

And with that final visit, my decision was made. As soon as we got into his car, I declared, "I want it." Justin smiled and said, "You got it."

Next came the offer (see Chapter 12). Justin was just as instrumental in helping me navigate this very nerve-racking process—both the semantics and the more emotional turbulence of it all. I didn't feel so alone in this after all.

THE 411

When deciding on your real estate agent, plan ahead to the sale. Negotiate up front with your real estate agent about what their commission cut will be. If you offer a win-win situation for them, they may be flexible with their payout. Consider a "lump-sum" deal if you are certain about your spending limit. This is a straight, agreed-upon commission with an incentive bonus (for example, $300) for every agreed-upon amount (say, $3,000) by which they are able to reduce the buying price.

The place cost $70,000 more than my limit, and it was still a sellers' market. Yet, as a smart and determined businesswoman, I trusted I could offer less than the asking price and still get it— especially because of a few other factors I'd learned about the property during our courtship, like the number of days it had already been on the market, and the fact that the seller was leaving the country in just a month to travel for a year (more on that in Chapters 12 and 13). However, I waffled on what the right number for the initial figure was. I didn't want to insult the seller and completely blow my game. And I didn't want to leave myself without any room to negotiate. I needed an expert opinion.

I nervously told Justin about the substantially lower figure I was thinking about offering. I was afraid he'd shake his head in disappointment. But, much to my surprise, he said, "I think it's a good starting number. I'll write up the offer and send it over to you within a couple hours."

This was yet another instance in which I felt fortunate to have carefully selected my real estate agent. Creating an offer-to-purchase contract can be a very daunting process. Because this world was completely foreign to me, I needed to be able to unequivocally trust my realtor to help educate and empower me about my rights, as well as about the ins and outs of writing the offer. Justin did just that.

We discussed all the details of the offer-to-purchase contract (see Chapter 12), including price, items in the home, escrow, repairs, possible loopholes through which we could back out, HOA fees, and so forth. Once every request and every possible contentious point had been exhausted, Justin sent the contract over to the selling agent, with our fingers crossed.

I waited eagerly. And I think Justin did, too. Maybe it was just due to the fact that we had really bonded, but I did feel like he cared—which was exactly what led me to have a panicky moment. My partnership with Justin would soon come to an end . . . and I'd be all alone in this endeavor. What if the seller refused my offer? Or what if I did get it? I was about to own a home all on my own. *Gasp!* I was freaking out.

An hour passed. Justin called. They had counteroffered. My nerves were on edge. I was still in the game, but I wasn't sure if I was relieved or more scared. Be careful what you wish for, indeed. I felt like I had fallen in love—I wanted this place desperately. But when what you want is in front of you like that, sometimes it feels safer to run from it. And that's exactly how I was feeling as the reality of paying a mortgage on my own was starting to sink in.

Justin consoled me about my jitters, though. I was on the verge of making the biggest decision in my life thus far. He was my rock. Between Justin and my mortgage broker, I felt supported, and the most confident I ever would, and I carefully reviewed the numbers and made sure I could afford to buy this place for a reasonable price.

Justin and I renegotiated. I gave him a number I thought was doable, feeling a bit more assured that I was actually in control of my destiny and doing the right thing. I rationalized the number by reminding myself that Justin's ongoing communications with the selling agent had revealed that I wasn't competing with another potential buyer for the home, and that they'd dropped the price quickly. So I felt confident in the offer I was proposing to my realtor. I had little choice in the matter, after all; I had surpassed my top-dollar amount and had very little wiggle room to play with, so I had to be willing to lose. But I didn't think I would this time. Aside from taking a more educated approach to my search and bidding process this time around, I had a very strong realtor negotiating on my behalf. I relied on that more than anything else.

Justin gently nudged me to offer a few thousand dollars more than the figure I'd suggested. His logic made sense, and I relented; he hadn't pushed me so far, so I trusted his judgment and expertise. I had to believe that he was in it for me.

We countered within the hour. "We," I say, as if Justin would be paying for half the mortgage. But that's how it felt—we were in it together.

My heart started racing again. Now they were in control. And letting someone else hold the key to my destiny—in this particular journey, anyway—was an uncomfortable feeling. But that was the reality of it, and I had to let go of my attachment to the outcome.

They had two days to respond.

Day one of the countdown began. Justin would occasionally call to let me know he hadn't heard anything yet. He was good like that; even when there was nothing to report, he let me know that. I needed it to maintain my sanity.

Day two came and went. Still no word. To take my mind off the pressure mounting inside my chest, I decided to go shopping. *Why not?* I justified it to myself. *It'll make me feel better, and*

clothes may be the last thing I get to buy in a long while if I get
the place.

Lunchtime passed. Justin called as I halfheartedly browsed
racks of shirts. No word. Again, he consoled me: "It's not necessarily bad," he said. "It means they're at least considering it."

The deadline to reject, accept, or counteroffer was quickly
approaching. The seller had only two hours left to respond. I was
losing my mind! I felt like I had been running a marathon and was
at the never-ending last mile—struggling uphill in the heat.

With just one hour remaining, Justin called. "Whatcha
doin'?" he asked. He sounded too nonchalant to have good news.
My stomach clenched.

"Eating sushi. I take it nothing, huh?" I said, disappointed.

"You're a homeowner. Congratulations."

I sat there, stunned. "Are you serious?"

"Most definitely," my loyal realtor and friend responded.

And that was only the beginning of what would become a long-
term friendship and partnership. Justin supported me fully
throughout the sale process, and called a team of people to help
me through escrow and inspections. Even after the transaction
was complete, he continued checking in with me. And, remember-
ing that he was my one-stop-shopping realtor, I still called upon
Justin for references for plumbers, painters, and the like. He never
failed to respond promptly—even months after the sale.

We've maintained our relationship; every now and then,
Justin calls me to ask how life is treating me. And I so appreciate
that he keeps me informed of what's going on in the local market

by sending me emails about real estate news. When the time comes for me to sell or buy again, my first call will be to Justin.

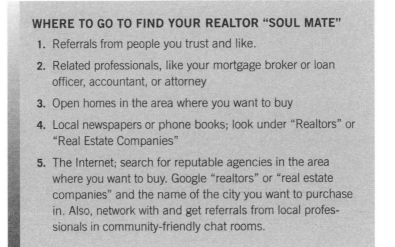

WHERE TO GO TO FIND YOUR REALTOR "SOUL MATE"

1. Referrals from people you trust and like.
2. Related professionals, like your mortgage broker or loan officer, accountant, or attorney
3. Open homes in the area where you want to buy
4. Local newspapers or phone books; look under "Realtors" or "Real Estate Companies"
5. The Internet; search for reputable agencies in the area where you want to buy. Google "realtors" or "real estate companies" and the name of the city you want to purchase in. Also, network with and get referrals from local professionals in community-friendly chat rooms.

You're a do-it-yourself girl? Good for you. In areas where I feel out of my league—like my finances, for which I have an advisor—I want an expert to hold my hand through the process. In the case of home hunting and buying, I wanted to avoid the hassle of being in charge of and alone with another project. This was one instance in which I accepted my vulnerabilities. I just wanted to be educated along the way and have the final say. A good leader, after all, delegates to a great support staff.

But if you prefer to be more hands-on and you have the time, I'm all for taking charge for yourself. Let your fingers do the walking, and investigate some of the online resources regarding property sales (noted in Chapter 11), and open homes in your area. Just don't sign any paperwork without letting an expert or an attorney review the contract for you.

eleven

Let the House Hunting Begin

B eing in charge of my life is a full-time job. Factor in writing, spending time with my friends and family, being the president of my homeowners' association, exercising, and doing basic life maintenance chores, and I am left depleted at the end of the week. Almost all the women I know feel the same way. Many of us have very little time left for ourselves to simply relax, read a book, try out a new recipe, or even take a "Calgon, take me away" bubble bath. And if you're a single mother, I'm sure your stress quadruples. You're probably reading this and chuckling, because to shout, "Oh, honey, you don't even have the first clue about what exhaustion feels like" will require too much energy— energy you need to attend to your kids, get the laundry done, and accommodate other people's needs.

Indeed, some of my most cherished memories in life have resulted from the flexibility and freedom I have because I'm single. I

don't have to worry about anyone else's agenda or feelings when
I want to book an exciting, last-minute trip to Puerto Vallarta or
Italy with my girlfriends. I can selfishly leave my bed unmade,
let clothes pile up in the laundry basket for weeks, or buy that
overpriced, low-cut dress that I'll only wear once a year but had
to have because I look so good in it.

Yes, in many ways, we single women—with or without
children—are very lucky. But I'd be lying to you if I didn't admit
that I sometimes wish I had a little help. There are days when I
think being single is the best thing in the world, and days when it's
practically unbearable. I'd like someone to get my car oil changed
before it burns up my engine; do the grocery shopping or the mil-
lion other small chores that start to feel overwhelming as they pile
up; or simply give me a hug after a long, hard day. My antidote
to this feeling is surrounding myself with people—friends, family members, or employees—who occasionally help out when I
need them.

I certainly considered this circumstance when deciding
which real estate agent I was going to work with. The last thing
I needed was more pressure in my life. I wanted to relegate work
to someone else, let them worry about the details. As long as I
was the decision maker, I was happy to employ someone else to
provide my options. Sure, doing so would come with a price. But
it was a nominal fee compared with the alternative cost: more
work for me.

By contrast, my unmarried but not unpartnered girlfriend
Jenel—a smart, twenty-eight-year-old professional who had been

dating her boyfriend, Mike, for nearly two years—decided that she would approach homebuying in the exact opposite way. She erroneously assumed that taking everything on by herself would be less traumatizing for her and Mike, who'd decided that they were ready to buy a place together.

Jenel had been maintaining her own apartment, which she shared with a roommate. However, because of the increasing amount of time she spent with her honey as their relationship flourished, Jenel's own space became little more than storage for her bedroom furniture . . . while she was all but installed at Mike's place. Eventually, their stockpiles of clothes and toiletries catalyzed the inevitable talk about the absurdity of paying two rents.

Should they or shouldn't they buy a home together? Would it be better for Jenel to move into Mike's apartment for the time being? Should they wait until they were engaged or married to buy a place as a twosome? Or should they just upgrade and go in on a bigger rental together? One thing was for sure: Mike and Jenel's conundrum gave her single girlfriends plenty to talk about as we tried to counsel her about her options. Meanwhile, Jenel and Mike diligently exhausted the pros and cons of each scenario. After weighing all the factors, they decided that plunging into housebuying felt like the best option for them at that time.

With their decision finalized, Jenel could finally take a deep breath and feel confident. I felt a tinge of jealousy, considering that I'd done it alone and she had a partner to go through the whole experience with. But little did Jenel know, she was in for quite a ride. As it would turn out, having someone to share the burdens of homebuying and owning with was not quite as comforting as she'd always fantasized it would be.

Mike, you see, is not much of a planner. He's more carefree, the opposite of Jenel, who's known for her analytical, orderly traits. He'd been a professional, sure, and was used to being responsible for paying his everyday living expenses, but he had never really developed a grand plan for the future.

After a month of talking it over, the topic of homebuying had faded into the backdrop of their everyday lives. It was becoming increasingly clear to Jenel that the only way this thing would happen would be if she took charge of it.

Jenel decided to initiate her and Mike's home-purchasing efforts by reviewing their combined financial situation. She was dismayed to learn that her adorably free-spirited boyfriend hadn't ever budgeted for a down payment on a home. (He was five years her senior, and she felt he should have planned accordingly.)

As it turned out, Jenel's house hunt wasn't much different from what I'd experienced as a single prospective buyer, because she ended up having to forge her path toward home ownership with much less support than she had originally anticipated.

After pushing through their financial fundamentals, Jenel nudged Mike into doing occasional "drive-bys" with her in neighboring communities, cruising for for-sale properties and open houses.

DRIVE-BYS

Scouting for-sale properties simply by driving through the neighborhoods you want to live in is known as doing "drive-bys." Most real estate agents will post signage the morning of an open house, announcing the time frame in which prospective buyers can view the property with the rest of the general public. Some real estate agents are even more proactive, and will post open-house information a few days before the event, in both the neighborhood and the local newspaper. Grab a pen and paper and jot down the addresses and times of the open homes you'd like to peruse.

It turned out that this experience was as cumbersome for Mike as a day of shopping at the mall. Jenel told me over drinks one night that it felt like dragging a child to church. For Mike, Sundays were all about watching golf on TV.

Although Jenel would have preferred a little more active participation and enthusiasm from Mike, she did appreciate his effort to join her when she made it clear to him how important it was to her. After all, he never asked her to spend Sundays watching sports, so she could appreciate his perspective. Still, she wanted him to be more involved. This was their future. *Doesn't he want to share in the excitement?* she wondered.

Enter the Internet. Mike's golf Sundays turned out to be just what Jenel needed to get him more involved. She decided to implement a new strategy: bringing her laptop to the couch while he watched TV, and pulling up listings in the areas and price range in which they wanted to buy.

Based on pictures and virtual tours on credible real estate websites that focused on properties for sale in the couple's area, Jenel compiled a list of homes she liked. When she'd gathered five or so, she would lean toward Mike and ask him to take a look. And without hesitation, he would oblige. Score! Jenel had succeeded in making house hunting more palatable for him.

When Jenel began employing this at-home house-hunting technique, Mike didn't have to move from the couch. He could get involved, voice his opinion, and make Jenel happy all at once—and with the comforting noise of the golf announcer in the background. Suddenly, house hunting didn't feel like such a chore for either of them.

Whether you've decided to employ a real estate agent or broker, or want to take the search into your own hands, familiarizing yourself with the current real estate landscape of the area you want to invest in is critical before you begin your search. Doing so will empower you to make a more educated purchase, both economically and aesthetically. You will learn quickly how to get the most bang for your buck. You will also learn whether your expectations are realistic. Here's how.

First things first: Go on a shopping spree! Like Jenel, dedicate one weekend day (weekends, particularly Sundays, are when realtors hold open homes for their clients) to simply touring homes in the neighborhoods you've determined you want to buy in. Let the shopping commence!

However, if you don't currently reside near the area you'd like to buy in, doing drive-bys to prep for homebuying is not much of an option. If this is the case, you'll especially want to rely on the Internet, which has opened the floodgates for many prospective homebuyers and sellers. They can now empower themselves with information about all things real estate—loans, up-to-date market value, and maintenance referrals. The Internet has become as essential to homebuying and selling as polished shoes are to a nicely tailored suit.

Through using the Internet, even a novice homebuyer can home in on some properties that may fit her wish list. And it can be fun! Once you familiarize yourself with sites that are credible in the real estate industry, it's like doing your shopping online. It's not as time consuming as drive-bys, and there's little to no sales pressure.

THE MATCH.COMS OF REAL ESTATE

1. Realtor.com: lists hundreds of homes for sale by multiple listing agents (MLSs). Realtor.com is sponsored by the accredited National Association of Realtors (NAR).

2. MLS.com: a membership-based site of realtors from various major cities across the country who come together to share buyer/seller information. It's free to search the MLS site for real estate—new and used homes; acreage; and land, commercial, and investment properties—for sale by MLS realty members in your area. The website also features real estate news, frequently asked real estate questions and answers, real estate classes, mortgage information, and mortgage information.

3. Ziprealty.com: a residential real estate brokerage firm. The company uses the Internet to enable homebuyers and sellers in major cities across the country to access comprehensive, local MLS home-listings data and other relevant information. By utilizing a technology platform, the company reduces costs for consumers.

4. Helpusell.com: an online service provider of professional, licensed real estate services nationwide that offers a set-fee alternative to paying the traditional broker commission.

5. Neighborhoodscout.com: a neighborhood search engine for homebuyers and a full-service real estate resource center. The site contains a large database of statistics about various neighborhoods nationwide that are revealed based on criteria you select.

6. Homes.com: an online destination for real estate listings of for-sale properties, new-home construction, foreclosures, and homes for rent. The site also allows you to research real estate agents from more than one brokerage firm in the area you're looking in.

7. Homeseekers.com: an ad-supported, national online service where you can find everything from homes for sale to agents to services that help you evaluate property.

8. Cyberhomes.com: provides public access to information about industry professionals, services, and technology, including an analysis of your home and community. Buyers and sellers can explore data ranging from property facts to value estimates to factors affecting the state of local and national housing markets.

9. BEA.DOC.gov: The U.S. Department of Commerce's website for its Bureau of Economic Analysis offers a plethora of state and local economic data to help you better gauge the current market value and growth potential of a given area.

10. Newspapervoyager.com: Check this website, sponsored by the Newspaper Association of America and listing small and large community newspapers nationwide, for a paper that's local to the area you want to buy in.

11. Zillow.com: a free, ad-supported online real estate service offering tools, data, information, and homes for sale by both realtors and owners.

12. Prudential, Sotheby's, and Coldwell Banker: nationally reputable real estate agencies.

Cyberspace is an amazing tool for helping you gather resources and information for homebuying. I would be remiss, however, if I did not forewarn you that relying solely on the Internet can create its own set of problems. Homebuying is a major investment, and one that should be undertaken with the same sound decision making as selecting a gynecologist. Blindly trusting online resources could gouge you financially.

BE A CYBERSLEUTH

1. Advertisements disguised as editorial content are biased.

2. Submitting personal information through unsecured sites puts you at risk of identity theft.

3. Sites are often sponsored by real estate industry organizations and professionals who may use your personal information to solicit your business.

4. Some sites are synched to related advertorial sites, and, with one click on a link, you may inadvertently be sent to the sponsoring site.

5. Some websites may ask you for an exclusive business contract or require membership. Be wary.

6. Smaller, online-only organizations often operate with limited budgets and are more prone to spontaneous bankruptcy than larger, corporation-backed sites.

7. Some sites that offer market-value information don't always factor in details, like a home's condition, yard size, and street parking, which might be important to you.

8. While online mortgage calculators compute loans that are affordable based on your salary, they do not factor in more personal ambitions, like saving money for going back to school for your PhD, or traveling for six months.

Local banks are often another resource for finding for-sale properties in neighborhoods where you'd like to reside. They are entrusted with lists of homes that are in, or are about to go into, foreclosure because the homeowners have defaulted on their loans. (Lenders have the right to take possession of a home in hopes of selling it to pay the balance of the mortgage.) An inexperienced homeowner should proceed with caution if she chooses to pursue a property that's been foreclosed on.

Searching for a home in this manner will be more time consuming for you. It can take months, even years, to find a property you like in this position. Once you do, a foreclosed property can unexpectedly get held up in the legal system, and can take longer to become available than you'd hoped. You're also subject to competing offers from professionals who invest in foreclosure properties to turn a profit. Potential lenders may also be more suspicious of foreclosed properties because of those homes' status.

Homeowners facing foreclosure are often at war with their lenders. It's not unheard of for embittered homeowners to destroy their homes before or on move-out day. These people may feel justified in bashing the property out of anger against the lender. They may even see the new homeowner as a scapegoat for their anger, and do unjust damage to the home just because they're feeling vindictive.

Another factor to consider regarding foreclosed properties is deferred-maintenance issues. Consider the likelihood that if the previous homeowners couldn't afford the monthly mortgage payment, they were probably not able to properly address plumbing, landscaping, painting, electricity, mold, insect problems, and other everyday considerations in running a home. You may also be faced with unpaid-property-tax debt. You will want to plan for both noticeable and undetected problems in foreclosure properties, and you may want to consider keeping a nest egg for remedying deferred-maintenance issues or unpaid debt.

It is true that foreclosed homes allow you to get more home for less money. Banks must attempt to recover the remaining balance (or the greatest amount they can) of the defaulted loan, and this scenario can put you in a prime position to buy a home for less than the current market value.

Newspapers are another way to search for available properties on your own. In smaller communities especially, they often list open homes or for-sale-by-owner properties, as well as pending foreclosures. Referrals from friends or professionals in related fields may also garner prospects for you. These options might take longer, but if you are not under any time constraints, they're worth investigating. Again, they may serve as a means of saving you money owed as commission to agents.

THE 411

For-sale-by-owner (FSBO—pronounced "fizbo") properties can save you big bucks in commission charges, since no real estate agent is serving as the middleman. However, consider the other advantages that agents can offer a novice homebuyer—escrow information, maintenance referrals, purchase contingencies, price negotiations, market value, and financial information—before sealing the deal on your own.

No matter how much you decide you want to be involved in your house hunt, here's a word to the wise: Do not participate in any sales transaction without consulting a professional first. Employing some sort of specialist on your behalf—like an attorney specializing in real estate matters, regardless of whether the seller has professional representation—is important. You want to have an expert who's looking out for your best interest. The seller's expert will have conflicting interests and is not the person whom you want to enlist. Now is not the time to cut corners and rely on an old-fashioned handshake to determine your financial destiny.

twelve

The Offer-to-Purchase Contract

m y friend Mina has been engaged twice. Fortunately, she didn't marry either of her former fiancés, both of whom brought her down. Born in Argentina, Mina moved to the United States in her early teens. Today she is a self-confident, independent, and successful thirty-three-year-old who's achieved many of her goals: She has a great job at a nationally acclaimed company, and she owns a two-bedroom condominium outside Los Angeles. She is beautiful and smart—the "total package."

"I never imagined my life would have played out like this," Mina told me, sounding contemplative. "When I was in my early and late twenties, I thought for sure I'd be happily married by now, living in a two- or three-bedroom home near my friends and family. My husband and I would regularly host barbecues at our humble home. We'd live carefree lives filled with travel, love, and adventure. Boy, did things play out differently!" Mina chuckled.

"In retrospect, I can honestly say that I was lucky I didn't end up with either of my fiancés. The engagement period was enlightening. I had every intention of getting married, both times. But the built-in time factor afforded by a proper engagement awakened me to some serious doubt and allowed me to back out before it was too late," Mina admitted.

"Honestly? Buying my condo, while daunting at the time, was ultimately easier and less frightening than deciding to spend the rest of my life with someone," she said unabashedly. "You can always sell your home if you need to. And there's a good chance you'll make money out of this investment. Investing in a marriage, well, your only out is divorce . . . and who wants that?"

Mina's candor was refreshing. And listening to her talk made me realize how much the offer on a house really is similar to an engagement period. Until both parties have signed on the dotted line, you're not tied to any agreement and can walk away virtually unscathed. You may be emotionally bruised, a little gun-shy, when it comes to going through the process again, but not the worse for wear. And you're sure to have gained some insight about how you want to go about things the next time, which is exactly how Mina is approaching her love life.

"Sure, I'd love to get married. But this time, I'm more focused on just finding a good fit for me. And when I do, I'll listen more closely to my gut before we get to the engagement stage, so when we do, it won't be so scary."

By now, you should know how much you have to spend on a home and what you have for a down payment. So now ask yourself this: *What am I willing to spend on this home?* The amount you decide on may not be what the seller thinks her home is worth. Therefore, you two must work to arrive at an agreement about what the property is worth, a price that is otherwise known as fair market value (FMV). The final sale price is a reflection of the fair market value of the property. However, before you negotiate that value with the seller (see Chapter 13), you will need to determine your offer and write up a contract accordingly. Several variables should be considered when determining what to offer for your first home.

THE 411

What is a comparable market analysis (CMA), or what's known in the real estate industry as a "comp"? A CMA offers home sale prices from the last six months for properties similar in age, size, location, and condition to the ones you're looking at. Comps paint an accurate picture of an area's landscape. Pay attention to sale prices versus asking prices. Higher asking prices in an area than what the comps reflect suggest an upswing in property value. Conversely, lower asking prices than what a property sold for in a comp reflect a declining market.

Now that you've fallen for this property enough to consider committing to it, ask your realtor for a written list of comps in the area. These will serve as a good starting point for deciding what your initial offer should be.

Obviously, your budgetary constraints can also inform your initial offer. By now, you should know what your top dollar is for any home. Is the seller's asking price in a range that allows you room to negotiate—either down (in a buyers' market) or up (in a sellers' market)—an amount that suits your personal budget?

THE 411

Keep in mind that escrow costs to close on a property, home inspections, and down payments are paid up front. Depending on what your budget is and how you negotiate your contract (see Chapter 13), you may want to consider all these variables when deciding your purchase price.

What about the property itself? Does it noticeably require any repairs? How much will they cost you? How about remodeling? Can you live with the home just the way it is for a while, or will you want to immediately knock down a wall and build an extra half-bath or repaint the exterior? Know in advance your general cost of any remodeling or obvious repairs, and factor that in when deciding your buying price.

GET A GOLD DIGGER

A reputable lender will likely require an official appraisal of the property before a sale can be finalized during escrow (see Chapter 15 for more on the escrow process). If the loan institution doesn't require such an appraisal, it's a smart idea to pay for one yourself. Finding flaws is an appraiser's job, and that person can spot potential issues that the novice's naked eye can't recognize. Getting an official appraisal also helps you determine what items will need fixing, so you can better assess the fair market value (FMV) of the property. But buyer beware: There's no need to splurge on a precontract appraisal. Your CMAs will guide your initial FMV offer. Write that you've approved an official property appraisal into the contract as a contingency for purchase (more on that later in this chapter).

Weigh the cost of appliances and utilities. Will your home come fully furnished, with a working oven/stove, refrigerator, dishwasher, and so on? Make sure you have enough additional money in case you need to buy something or a major appliance breaks down. Otherwise, you might end up in the position my friend Samantha found herself in when, after purchasing her home, complete with a brand-new washer and dryer, she discovered that a plumber would need to install a device to make them actually work. Is there a working fireplace or swimming pool in the home you want to buy? What kind of maintenance has been done or needs to be done to make them work properly, and how much will it cost you? And, of course, what kind of monthly utility and maintenance expenses are you looking at to keep your home running smoothly?

If your first home is a shared-living space, like a condo or a co-op, determining what additional monthly fees you will be paying is essential before you finalize your purchase price. The set amount should be taken into consideration when you make your offer, to ensure that you can cover all your expenses without suffering. Also remember to add some wiggle room for extra expense in case the building's association determines it needs to raise your monthly fees or imposes a special assessment charge.

THE 411

An association for a shared-living space can levy a special monthly assessment charge—which homeowners often vote on—to cover a large expense that your predetermined monthly fees do not account for. Depending on your state laws, a special assessment fee can last for a couple of months or for decades, and its amount can vary widely. Often, reading the publicly posted minutes of an association's meeting will help you anticipate any hikes in monthly fees or an imposed special assessment. Or you can be resourceful, find the association president's name and contact information where it's posted in a common area, and inquire about the complex's future.

Also account for how hot the current market is in your desired area. How long are homes staying up for sale? If they're going like hotcakes, your offer is going to need to be more competitive. As I mentioned earlier, comps are a good way to gauge the recent market value in a given area. But to determine your bargaining power for the specific home that your heart desires, ask your realtor how many days the property has been on the market (this information is abbreviated as DOM on real estate documents). If the market is hot, the DOM should be low, and you may need to ante up with a competitive price. Depending on why the seller is selling, if the DOM reflects that the property has been on the market for sixty days or more, you may be able to use that information to your advantage and offer a lower-than-normal price. The seller could be antsy to sell.

Speaking of the seller, it's a good idea to get a glimpse of her story. Homebuying, after all, can be an intensely personal and emotionally charged time for both the seller and the buyer. Do your best to minimize your stress or anxiety about making an offer on a home, and try not to let your offer reflect your emotions, because—let's face it—you're probably scared and nervous. Instead, use that energy to help you remain levelheaded about the whole process. Also, in a situation in which both people have something the other person needs or wants, you're likely to strike a better deal if you consider the seller's perspective. The smartest negotiators are those who make their opponent feel as if they're winning, too, even if they're not. (See Chapter 13 for more on negotiations.)

Rarely, however, are you in a position to meet the seller personally before negotiations begin. So inquire about her life—start with your agent, then move on to hers. Specifically, find out why she's selling, where she's going, and whether the house has a history that pertains to the individual. Arming yourself with this information might offer good insight into how motivated she will be to sell, as well as other considerations that might make you the buyer she'll want to consider.

In my case, my friendly investigative work awakened me to a potential cost-saving opportunity when the seller's agent divulged why the seller was selling: She was leaving her job the following month to travel internationally with her fiancé for a year, whether her home sold or not. Bingo! I put myself in her shoes and determined: *If I were her, I wouldn't want to deal with the hassle of a subletter or a sale while I was traversing Europe with my sweetheart.* I was confident that this nugget of information could work in my favor down the line.

Time was also on my side. It was December; Christmas was approaching. The holiday months of November, December, and January are not opportune times for sellers to put their homes on the market. Money tends to be a bit scarcer for people around this time, as they overextend their budgets to buy holiday presents and travel to celebrate with their families and friends. And with tax season just around the corner, people tend to reevaluate their spending habits and review their budgets in preparation for Uncle Sam's knock on their door. This pattern translates into buyers' having fewer competing offers to contend with, and the possibility of dealing with a more eager seller.

If you're contemplating making an offer during the winter, don't forget that tax season is right around the corner for you, too. Just because you're buying a house doesn't mean the IRS won't want its share of your money that year. And what you ultimately pay for the property is a key variable in the amount of your yearly property taxes. So, whether you alleviate the property-tax burden by paying twelve monthly installments or pay twice-yearly lump sums, make sure you have enough money to cover this expense when determining your offer price.

Finally, be sure to leave yourself enough excess funds to negotiate with. Rarely do most initial offers stick. Typically, a homeowner will counteroffer. (This is the process in which the seller considers all aspects of your offer-to-purchase contract and proposes her own set of stipulations for the sale, including a new sale offer based on your initial offer.)

Making your initial offer on your purchase price is much like agreeing on your initial salary when you take a job. It generally becomes the foundation on which your company bases your pay increases as you move up the corporate ladder. Take into account all the potential variables above before deciding on the number from which all your negotiations will originate.

Once you've cemented your purchase price with your real estate agent, he'll write up an offer-to-purchase contract, the official document that clearly states you want to buy the property. It also serves as the document that identifies what the seller is selling and at what costs.

THE LOWDOWN

Know the difference between a low offer and lowballing! If you're buying during a market period that allows for offering an amount below the asking price, proposing a low offer is a smart strategy. A seller and her agent will intuitively know you're leaving the door open for further negotiations. Lowballing a seller, on the other hand, is offensive and could completely turn her off. Remember—while homebuying is a business transaction, someone's home is a very proud, private space that often breeds emotional attachment. Lowballing a potential seller is insulting; it suggests that either you don't think her home is valuable, or you're simply trying to take advantage of her. Lowballing could cause you to lose a deal even before the deal making gets started.

In addition to the actual price you're willing to pay for the home, a purchase contract will include a number of stipulations about details you'd like the seller to attend to before you buy. Again, think of it as if you're negotiating a work contract, where you build in additional vacation time, bonuses, work-from-home options, and more. Items like repairs, material assets and appliances, and monthly condominium fees are negotiable options in a purchase contract. Make sure to write your entire wish list into the initial offer, no matter how absurd it seems. A seller can always take it off the table in her counteroffer.

PICK AND CHOOSE YOUR BATTLES: EIGHT NEGOTIABLE AREAS TO CONSIDER WHEN DRAFTING YOUR PURCHASE CONTRACT

1. Amenities
2. Furniture
3. Repairs
4. Escrow charges and representation
5. Property taxes
6. HOA dues and fees
7. Maintenance *and* maintenance fees
8. Move-in date/escrow period

Loopholes, otherwise referred to as "contingencies" in the real estate business, are also factored into the purchase contract. Contingencies are requirements that the buyer establishes in a purchase contract that must be fulfilled before the sale is complete. They're your safeguard if you have to back out of the purchase. However, don't waste a seller's time by writing a litany of outlandish contingency requests into your purchase contract. And if you're scared—which is completely normal—don't throw up numerous contingency "barriers" to keep the sale from taking place. As with falling in love, if you're not ready to commit, then you shouldn't get engaged! Use contingencies only as a means of rescinding your offer if your requirements aren't met in a manner that's acceptable to you.

THREE STANDARD CONTINGENCIES

1. The seller's financial backing is approved.
2. You accept all home-inspection reports.
3. You have the right to review and approve the property's title report or the master deed's bylaws and budget.

If you're not satisfied with the outcome of any of the contingencies listed in your offer-to-purchase contract, it does not mean your deal is dead in the water. It's up to you to decide if you want to move forward with renegotiating the terms of your purchase contract (see Chapter 13), based on the seller's response.

Your purchase contract will also reflect the details of your financial support, showcasing to the seller your ability to close the deal. The purchase contract should be based on realistic loan terms—hopefully, you've already prequalified or been preapproved for a loan at this point. Your real estate agent should use this information to prove that you're committed to going through with the sale.

The papers are all drafted. It's time to sign your offer. Breathe. This is probably the scariest thing you've encountered in a long time. You probably feel both excited and overwhelmed by fear. From what I'm told, homebuying is a lot less excruciating than childbirth! So give yourself a break; things could be worse.

During this process, you may be saying to yourself, *I can't believe I'm doing this!* Or, if you're more like me, you may be thinking, *Let's just get it over with!* Just know that whatever happens, you'll be okay.

TILL DEATH DO YOU PART

The purchase agreement is a legally binding contract. Consider having an attorney review and approve it, and make that a clause in your contract within a few days of the seller's acceptance of your offer. Also write a clause into your contract that clearly states that contingencies must be removed to your satisfaction before the sale is complete.

Remember, you've done your homework. If this home is meant for you, it will work out okay in the end. And if not, something more suitable is out there for you.

thirteen

Negotiating and Counteroffering

I admit it: I read my horoscope daily . . . and I often twist, turn, and stretch my interpretation of it to make astrology accurately predict my future. I've had my birth chart done, my tarot cards read, a numerologist forecast my year ahead. Still, my numerous and varied attempts to quiet my restless heart about the unknown have served only as illusory moments of consolation. And while I'd love to believe that the stars must align before I can get everything I want, I know that I actually have a big say in determining my future. True, I can't ask the planets to shift and then—*poof!*—I'll collide with my Mr. Right or the perfect job, but there is one thing I know for certain: The universe didn't determine my hand in homeowning. That was all me.

When you draw up the purchase contract, your homeowning fate is in the palm of your hand. Now the seller must consider

the price and the terms of your agreement to buy. Welcome, my
friend, to the negotiation process.

KEEP IT SIMPLE

Focus your energy on getting a signed offer by narrowing your
negotiations to major selling points, like price and closing issues
or other glaring considerations. Without a signed contract, a seller
can sell out from under you. Before you realize it, you've lost the
negotiations before they've even begun. Escrow is the time to
work out financial glitches in your mortgage, or minor inspection
issues. If you don't approve of the inspection findings, you can
renegotiate or drop out. If your financing falls through, you're not
out any money—just the home.

"Negotiating is a wait-and-see game," says Cathy, a thirty-
eight-year-old Michigan native who has purchased one condo and
one freestanding single-family home as a single woman. "It's empowering, exhilarating, and draining all in one."

Cathy asserts that her condo was the best investment she ever
made. In just a few years, she made $300,000. She bought at a
good time, but her negotiations were really what made this deal
possible. The seller agreed to pay closing costs (nearly $5,000
alone) and reduced the purchase price to cover some minor repairs. "Truthfully," Cathy confesses, "I'd have taken the place
even if the seller hadn't fixed the minor stuff. It was a gamble,
and I won!"

A seller will review your contract and likely reply with her own written proposal, called a counteroffer. The seller can negotiate most anything, including price, contingencies, and escrow details—things like selecting an escrow officer or determining when you'll take possession of the home.

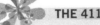

THE 411

Escrow happens when both parties have agreed to the terms of the contract, and begins when all signed and pertinent contracts and documents are delivered to a third party known as an escrow officer. The escrow officer finalizes the deal between the seller and the buyer. Escrow includes filing documents with the government reflecting the pending sale, and clearing title, homeowners' insurance premiums, corrective work credits, and inspection fees for the final sale of a home.

For the most part, if you receive a counteroffer, consider it a good sign. Typically it means the seller thinks what you're requesting is somewhat reasonable. It also means you're competitive with any other offers she may have on the table. Translation: You're still in the game. Take a deep breath. This is when it gets exciting!

In my case, my purchase price was approximately $25,000 less than the seller's asking price. The seller immediately dropped her asking price by $10,000 in her counteroffer. Bingo! She was ready to play ball.

She also requested that escrow close sixteen days after signing. Uh-huh—another sign she was motivated to sell. First I had found out that the very next month, my seller was quitting her job and traveling abroad for a year. And now, by dropping her price dramatically within a couple hours of my initial offer and wanting a quick escrow period, she obviously wanted to make this sale happen. I had snagged her attention. *Now I have room to wheel and deal,* I thought.

I agonized about the price. Her counterprice was still $59,000 over the limit I'd given myself, but I knew what was out there. If I could talk her down a bit more, I was willing to stretch my budget.

The tight closing period was not an issue for me. I was in a month-to-month lease in a rent-controlled apartment. My roommate had already agreed to move in and pay rent wherever I chose to buy. I was all set to rock and roll. I would concede to the closing date if the seller would compromise on the price. She had agreed to all of my other contingencies, so there was nothing else outstanding. Now it was my turn at bat.

With little room to move on the price, I rolled the dice and agreed to the tight turnaround. But I only upped my offer by $6,000. Justin seemed a little skeptical, but he didn't push me. We weighed the list of pros and cons, and we determined that we definitely had a motivated seller on our hands. Compared with the seller's counterprice and the going market, my offer was still a little low. It was not, however, a lowball offer. It was still respectable.

With my offer in, now my gut was in knots. I'd reached the point of no return. My offer made it clear that I wasn't budging much on the price. If the seller wanted to unload her pride and joy, she'd have to meet my needs. I was, after all, meeting hers.

THE LEG UP

Unless it's a hot sellers' market, the buyer is usually in the prime position in negotiations. Sellers often look to unload their properties due to emotionally charged, changing circumstances. Reasons like relocation, financial constraints, a growing family, death, divorce, and marriage can work in the buyer's favor because finessing these types of circumstances with ease often depends on the sale of the seller's home.

As you will recall from Chapter 10, my seller waited until just one hour before the deadline to respond that she'd agreed to my purchase price. I later learned that she'd been reluctant to acquiesce to my price, partly because it meant that she wouldn't get as much as she'd expected, and partly out of pride. Apparently, she thought my minimal counterprice meant I was just trying to "win" the negotiations.

TIME'S A-TICKIN'

An offer-to-purchase contract is usually laden with deadlines and other items like contingency removals, close of escrow, and deposit increases. Take them seriously, as you are legally bound by them upon signing the contract. However, if you note in advance that you need more time, a realtor may be a little bit flexible. His main objective, after all, is to sell the property. Unless there are competing offers to consider, flexing to your time constraints a bit will only behoove the seller.

But my realtor had convinced her realtor, and accurately so, that I really was stretched financially; I wasn't trying to take advantage of her. As was revealed afterward, what helped sway her decision to sell to me, despite my low offer, was the emotionally appealing handwritten letter I'd submitted to her with my original purchase offer.

I opened my note to the seller by complimenting her home and decorating taste, but from a heartfelt, genuine place, not as if I were just pumping her up. I followed that with revealing a little bit about myself, my life, and how I simply fit into her home. And I ended the letter by wishing her well on her new life journey abroad. I thanked her for taking the time to read the letter, and for considering me for the job of taking good care of her home.

YOU CAN CRY IF YOU WANT TO

People often grow attached to their homes and the memories they've created there. Sometimes, writing a seller an authentic, personal letter from the heart—expressing why you want the home, and how you'll take care of it as lovingly as she has—is just the sales tool to push a seller over the edge, especially in a competitive market. Submit your letter with your initial offer to purchase. It could mean the difference between thousands of dollars in negotiations and clinching your victory over a less conscientious homebuyer, even one with more money to spend.

In the end, my seller and I were both victorious. She received a competitive dollar amount, she didn't have to deal with any repairs, and she got all her escrow requests met, including an uncommonly quick, sixteen-day closing time frame. Meanwhile, I got my home. Ultimately, I believe it was my win-win negotiating style, not a take-no-prisoners approach, that won my seller over.

Negotiating is a life skill. Life, after all, is dependent on relationships with others—whether in love, friendship, or business. Everyone negotiates differently, and different situations sometimes call for different negotiation styles, depending on factors that stack the odds either in your favor or against you.

According to *Home Buying for Dummies,* people tend to employ one of two types of negotiation styles: competitive or cooperative. A competitive negotiation style means someone wins and someone loses; a cooperative negotiator solves problems, rather than defeating, so both sides give a little but win, too.

Neither style is right or wrong. Your approach to purchasing your home depends on numerous variables (outlined in Chapter 12), including your personality, the market, and the seller's personality. Don't forget that real estate agents highly influence the negotiation of a sale as well, like Justin did in my purchase. He knew how to finesse the selling agent with the right information to encourage her to take note of my concessions.

THE C-WORDS

A competitive negotiation style is usually only tolerated by either party when the market is heavily weighted toward either a seller or a buyer. In a more balanced market, however, competitive negotiating is often a turnoff (barring any drastic variables, like relocation or foreclosures, that require the immediate sale or purchase of a home), and a cooperative style is more effective.

Remember my friend Cathy? Thanks to her savvy negotiation skills when she purchased her condo, as well as a rising sellers' market, she made a killing when it came time to sell. But leaving her place forced her to be a buyer as well—a position in which she didn't have room to wheel and deal. As a seller she did great, but as a buyer she had to face a sellers' market and contend with new circumstances.

"It was an exciting time for me," she told me. "I was newly engaged, feeling good about my smart investment as a single woman, and thrilled to be starting this new journey with my fiancé. So when my fiancé and I found our dream starter home, we wasted no time in the negotiations."

Cathy learned early on that the house she and her fiancé wanted had just fallen out of escrow with another buyer, so the seller was wary of selling to anyone who didn't seem serious in their offer-to-purchase contract. Cathy realized that they needed to go in strong and impress the seller, who'd made it clear that she would be calling all the shots. "There was no question we wanted the house," says Cathy.

They offered the seller's asking price and waived every contingency they legally could. The seller had disclosed numerous items in need of repairs, but Cathy felt that she and her fiancé could rely on the home inspection to inform them of any circumstances that would threaten their safety or drain them financially. As long as the home proved to be structurally sound overall, they were willing to incur the expense of replacing or repairing whatever wasn't working. (I wouldn't normally recommend doing what they did— it can be costly—but buyers may choose to take this approach when they want to seem like attractive prospects to the seller.) For Cathy and her fiancé, it worked. They were victorious over other bidders whose asking prices were slightly higher, but whose contracts were layered with contingencies.

"And wouldn't you know it?" Cathy tells me. "After all that, my fiancé and I broke up shortly thereafter." Fortunately, only her name was on the title. "I had used the profit from my condo to pay for the down payment. I didn't think it was fair for him to be entitled to all I'd worked so hard for as a single woman. Thank goodness I didn't let love blind me!"

Cathy kept the place and made it work on her own. After all, when you enter into any business transaction, you need to prepare for a few stumbling blocks. When deciding her purchase price, Cathy had silently weighed the idea that her fiancé might not always be in the picture, and that by law, he wasn't responsible for any of the mortgage, since the loan was solely in her name. With that, Cathy smartly offered a conservative enough number to leave room in her finances to protect her and her credit for that "just-in-case" moment. Turns out that her business savvy—and her gut—were right.

fourteen

Detecting and Inspecting Potential Problems

You're almost an official homeowner! Can you believe it? Now's the time to closely examine your future abode for flaws if you haven't done so already. There are some simple tests you can do that don't require a plumber or an electrician. You can and should scour your home for blemishes that are noticeable to the naked eye.

BE A SUPER SLEUTH: TWELVE AREAS TO INVESTIGATE ON YOUR OWN

1. Toilet: Does it flush properly? Does it run afterward?
2. Lights and light switches: Are they working, or do they flicker?
3. Kitchen appliances: Does the stove heat up? Is the microwave working? Do the refrigerator and freezer

167

temperatures feel right? Is the dishwasher newer and in good condition? How about the garbage disposal? Is it making any funky noises?

4. Water faucets: How's the water pressure in the shower or bathtub? Does the kitchen sink's faucet leak?

5. Drains: Are any of the sinks, tubs, or showers backed up? Check any community areas for such problems, too.

6. Washer and dryer: Does the dryer heat up? Does the washer work? How are they maintained? And how does the supporting ventilation system seem?

7. Windows and doors: Do they open and close with ease? What condition are the screens in? Do they lock and unlock properly? Do you feel secure?

8. Peculiar smells: Where are they emanating from and what's the cause? Moisture, mold, or gas leaks could be lurking, and that's not good.

9. Structure and foundation: What kinds of materials were used—quality or cheap? Do walls and doors slope, or are they level? Are there cracks or unfilled holes? Are repair jobs noticeable or undetectable to a novice? Are any tiles buckling? How does the roofing look?

10. Discoloration or spots: Water leaks can create spots, buckling, and discoloration. Do you notice any such flaws in your home and/or any common areas?

11. Insect issues: Have you checked the foundation for deterioration? Wood and stucco homes are highly susceptible to termite problems. Check behind, between, and underneath hard-to-reach areas like washer and dryers, refrigerators, and so on. How clean is the overall condition of the home? Filth encourages bug infestation. Look near community trash and recycling.

12. Ground: What is your house built on and around? If it's in a hilly area, know its mudslide vulnerability. Are you in swamp territory? How's the community's waste and drainage system? Are you on a fault line? Look for earthquake damage.

Thirty-six-year-old Emily is a carpenter's daughter. When Emily decided to buy a house in Seattle, she asked her dad, who lived in the Midwest, to coach her on potential problems to look for when she was house hunting. Emily didn't want to be blindsided by whopping repair costs caused by unseen percolating issues.

Emily's dad wouldn't be able to fly out to check out every potential site, so she felt the weight of having to fend for herself. Knowing the importance of this stage of the game, Emily was intimidated. She needed to find someone she could trust. Emily had learned from her father at an early age that maintenance is critical to a home's upkeep. The last thing she wanted was to buy a home that required a lot of repair work. She didn't have the energy, resources, or finances to deal with it. But before Emily could start her search for an inspector, she needed to know what to look for.

First, knowing the different types of essential home inspections is important because you don't want to be taken for a ride by either the seller or a home inspector. Interior, exterior, and pest-control inspections are critical means of letting you know what you're getting yourself into—and, most important, if you want to stay there. If you're buying a fixer-upper, then you'll also want the expert opinion of a general contractor or architect, who can judge the structural foundation of your would-be home.

An inspection of the interior and exterior of your freestanding single-family home, co-op, condo, town home, or duplex includes a thorough examination of the plumbing, electrical work, heating and cooling systems, kitchen, bathroom, insulation, smoke detectors, and more. Remember, the inspector is there to uncover the issues you can't detect because doing so is not your forte. Much in the way a financial advisor helps you investigate the best ways to invest your money, an inspector will guide you with information that helps you protect your potential real estate investment.

THE 411

There are two types of home defects. A defect that's visible to a potential homebuyer, like a crack or leak, is a patent defect. Even patent defects should be checked by an inspector. You will want to know the origin and the extent of the damage, since those details can seriously impact contract renegotiations. Latent defects are the second type of home issues—only a home inspector can detect them. Latent defects are problems that are concealed in inaccessible areas—such as the furnace and water pipes—and may pose a health and safety problem, like gas leakage. Fraudulent title claims and zoning deficiencies are also latent defects that experts can expose.

If you're buying in a shared-living complex, ask your inspector to provide you with an overall analysis of the building's structure. The inspector may detect potential problems like drain and sewer issues, roofing concerns, or termites—all of which affect your complex and could become detrimental to you. Ask the selling realtor for access to key areas of the complex, like the boiler room, garage, and roof. These areas generally house the most potentially costly problems, ones that even a homeowners' association may not have discovered yet.

THE 411

Property inspectors are generalists, and their services cost between $250 and $650. If extensive damage becomes apparent, a good inspector will refer you to a specialist in areas like insects, roofing, and structure.

A thorough insect inspection is equally important in gauging your future home's durability. You'd be surprised at the damage those little creatures can cause to your home if problems are not caught in time or are left untreated. Warm or damp climates in particular are breeding grounds for termites, ants, and beetles. They also cause structural and hygienic issues like dry rot, mold, and fungi—precisely the kinds of environments in which bugs thrive.

My homeowners' association faced our own insect debacle just a year and a half after I purchased my condo. While my unit checked out fine during the inspection stage, my complex's foundation suffered from severe deferred maintenance and poor workmanship, which were unnoticeable to me as a newbie home-owner. Much to my chagrin, I didn't think to ask my inspector his opinion about the condition of the overall complex.

The former association's poorly managed earthquake-repair job, coupled with their short-term-cost-savings mentality, ended up emptying our association's reserve funds and draining me emo-tionally. As it turned out, the wood used to reconstruct portions of the building's structure ten years earlier hadn't been chemically treated to resist water or termite damage. Subsequently, it had severely eroded from water leakage over the years. And then—bingo!—we were living in an easy target for termite infestation.

As president of the association, I was bequeathed the task of leading my board of directors, on behalf of sixty-nine homeown-ers, through a massive, summerlong, $90,000 reconstruction of the building's foundation.

The project was a major but necessary inconvenience for us homeowners, who didn't have access to our elevator for two months. Hauling groceries up and down stairs was frustrating and tiring, particularly for the complex's elderly residents. Meanwhile, homeowners trying to sell or sublet their units had a difficult time doing so with the building in such disarray.

The construction was also a financial burden. In order to pay for the unexpected expense and still be able to make headway on other deferred-maintenance issues like painting, each homeowner incurred an additional $100 a month in special assessment fees for twelve months. And when you're already struggling to make your mortgage payment, an extra $100 a month can leave you feeling pretty strapped.

THE 411

Pest-control inspectors charge from $200 to $500 and should be consulted when your overall interior and exterior inspection happens. Many inspectors are qualified to perform both types of inspections.

Okay, now that you know what a property inspector does, you'll want to begin your hunt for a good one *before* you need him. Like searching for a good mortgage broker or real estate agent, selecting a reputable and trustworthy property inspector is very important.

Emily learned that the hard way. She found herself in the position of wanting to move on a home without having an inspector in place. She was out of her comfort zone and under a time crunch. Her contract gave her seventy-two hours to get her home inspected and write up any revisions to the contract, based on the inspector's findings regarding the home's condition.

Emily didn't have the first clue about where to find, or what to look for in, a reputable property inspector. With her deadline in her contract fast approaching, she panicked.

Fortunately, Emily had a great real estate broker, who came to the rescue with his own little black book of resources. Though Emily was not obligated to use one of the inspectors her realtor referred her to, she also didn't have the time to do a thorough search for an inspector herself. Between work, caring for her puppy, and reconfiguring her finances for her looming mortgage, Emily was exhausted. Since she'd grown to respect and trust her realtor, Emily took the easy path and hired an inspector her realtor recommended.

THE 411

Good realtors have good relationships with all types of people in the industry. Before employing one of their references, you should know what to look for and be certain you like the person's work style. Some realtors make deals with various real estate vendors and receive compensation for recommending their services to buyers. Ask your realtor if she does. And make sure to interview your inspector yourself before you hire them. It's one of your smartest negotiations for protecting your finances.

Fortunately, Emily's realtor's inspector was on top of his game. He kindly detailed for her what he was doing as he went along, and educated Emily about what the norm was regarding predictable defects, and which ones might be dangerous, in any area he worked through. The inspector followed up with a written report and invited Emily to call if she thought of any last-minute questions.

In the end, Emily lucked out with an almost flawless home and no major repair expenses to contend with. Two days later, her escrow went through without a hiccup, and Emily became the proud owner of her first two-bedroom home, all by her lonesome.

But you can't count on having the type of luck Emily had in your own home inspection. Finding a credible property inspector can be tough. Many states don't require inspector licensing. So you're more likely to be left relying on an interview and your instincts to distinguish a dud from a quality person. Also, hiring a general contractor, engineer, or architect to inspect your property doesn't give you the full scope of potential problems. Plus, this person could be hoping to do any repair jobs your property may require, or may try to suck you into an unnecessary remodeling project. Trusting someone who may have ulterior motives is never a good idea, of course, but how will you know the difference?

First, ask people you know and trust (like friends, your realtor, or coworkers) for referrals. The American Society of Home Inspectors (ASHI) also lists certified and licensed home inspectors in various regions who have had to pass two written proficiency exams and perform at least 250 property inspections in order to become ASHI members. Visit www.ashi.com or call 800-743-2744 to find a list of esteemed property inspectors in your area.

You can always check out "Building, Home, or Property Inspection Services" in the time-tested Yellow Pages. But keep in mind that some inspectors may list membership in other professional associations that don't require continuing education or adhere to a high standard of practice.

TOP TEN QUESTIONS TO ASK A POTENTIAL PROPERTY INSPECTOR

1. *What areas do you cover in your inspection?* A good inspector will examine your would-be home from roof to foundation, inside and out.

2. *Are you licensed, and by whom? Are you certified in any specific areas?*

3. *Do you carry errors and omissions insurance?* In case a property inspector misses an expensive problem, errors and omissions insurance protects the inspector and you from incurring the cost of getting it fixed.

4. *Is this your full-time job? About how many inspections do you do in a year?* The more, the better, particularly in the area in which you wish to buy. The inspector will be more familiar with local problems and zoning, and you can ask for neighbors' references.

5. *How long has your company been in business?* You want someone who's an expert, and who has a sound professional history. Check the local Better Business Bureau for bad reports.

6. *How long before you can come, and how long will the inspection take?* Under a deadline, availability is key.

A thorough examination may last an hour and a half to three hours.

7. *How much do you charge, and what is that price based on?* Remember, cheaper isn't always better. A quality home inspector will save you oodles of money in the long run. Property inspectors should have a base price; watch out for inspectors who charge based on the time they spend on-site. If they discover a problem that requires extra attention, they need to let you know before tacking it on to your bill. Note: Generally, you're required to pay for the inspector's service upon completion of the examination.

8. *How do you summarize your findings?* Protect yourself! You want a written report specific to your property's mechanical and structural condition. Ask up front for sample reports from other home inspections this person has conducted.

9. *Does your report detail repair costs?* Inspectors aren't repairpeople and shouldn't be relied on to provide the cost of repairing a defect in your home. Inspectors may, however, refer you to several people who might be able to give you a general estimate for a typical home repair.

10. *May I, my agent, and the selling agent be present during the inspection?* It's your investment and your business to be in the know. You'll also want all representing agents to be present at the inspection, since they're on the front lines of any renegotiations for closing the deal.

Review your home inspection report thoroughly, and don't be shy about calling and asking your inspector for clarity—in laymen's terms. This just may be your last way out of a potential money pit. Now is not the time to gloss over details.

Keep in mind, however, that a property inspection report exists to detect more expensive property damage, so don't ask the seller to ante up for obvious but unsightly issues, like a hole in the hardwood floor, carpet stains, or a broken garbage disposal, that should have been broached in your initial offer-to-purchase contract. Use the inspection report to renegotiate the sale price to account for unforeseen and costly damages.

REQUIRE PROTECTION

Whenever possible, attempt to negotiate that the seller pay for a home warranty or protection plan that covers some of your home's major systems and appliances. Just because your home passes an inspector's examination at the time of purchase doesn't mean things aren't going to break in the future. A home warranty or protection plan is an added bonus, and, for a deductible of between $25 and $50 per visit, it may keep you from having to plunk down $800 you don't have toward the purchase of a new refrigerator.

Can you believe you've made it this far? *Hold on!* You're almost an official homeowner.

fifteen

ESCROW AS A SECOND LANGUAGE
Learning How to Talk Dirty

When I was in the process of negotiating the purchase contract for my first home, I couldn't stop thinking about it. I was on edge and out of my element, and I turned to anyone who'd listen as a way to release my anxiety.

Sherry, a friend of mine from Texas, was visiting during my negotiations and was supportive as I vented over dinner. Sherry understood the emotional duress I was under. She'd bought her first home solo in Texas only a year and a half earlier.

But the more I talked to Sherry about my experience, the more I started to second-guess myself. Admittedly, I didn't really know what I was doing. I was learning as I went along, relying on my realtor's advice, my friends' and acquaintances' opinions, and my intuitive business sense to guide me through the process—tactics that definitely were not sufficient.

Sherry knew a lot about real estate. She started pontificating about escrow and titles and deeds. She might as well have been speaking a foreign language. I'd heard the terminology, of course, but I didn't have a solid understanding of what it all entailed. I feigned interest. Really, though, she was making me even more stressed out than I already was.

Sherry, it turned out, had lost out on her first-choice property during escrow. Her financing had fallen through unexpectedly, and within hours the deal was dead in the water. Her mishap had left her emotionally scarred. But she gathered her wits and kept on with her search, and she ended up with the delightful two-bedroom home she owns now.

I wasn't too far into my search for a new home when I learned how much people love to give advice about homebuying, whether you ask for it or not. It's not unlike unsolicited advice about weddings or raising children; there just seem to be certain topics around which people have zero self-control. The problem, of course, is that they often project their own experience—or lack thereof—onto you and your situation. And you're left to pick up the pieces and decipher what's worth paying attention to and what is most definitely not your concern.

The best advice I can give to you, my reader and sister in single power, is when it comes to escrow, read on! Take it from me: The more you know about the escrow process and terminology, the more secure and empowered you will feel during this otherwise tenuous phase.

Okay, first, just what *is* the anatomy of an escrow? It starts as one of many out-of-pocket cash expenses that you need to be prepared for before you've finalized the sale of your home, but your real participation in the process begins when you give all your homebuying documents, contracts, funds, and instructions to a neutral third party, your escrow officer. At the end of escrow, your escrow officer will have tallied your true final bill of sale, as well as filed all the documents that legally prove you are the new homeowner.

THE 411

The legal document that clearly states who owns a home is called a title. (It may also loosely be referenced as a deed of trust in some states depending on the terms of sale.) An escrow officer prepares paperwork related to legally transferring the title from one homeowner to another. Title transference requires proper signatures, timely deliveries, and the pending sale–made-public record. It also requires an escrow officer to review compliance with lending instructions, including any title insurance requirements (see Chapter 3) and general accounting matters.

Upon negotiating and signing your offer-to-purchase contract, you may have agreed upon who will be your escrow representative. An escrow firm, lawyer, or title company are all options when it comes to who might represent you. Sometimes a seller will want to use her escrow officer of choice to assure a smooth and timely transaction. You have nothing to lose by going along with this.

For certain, you or your seller will have a preference regarding when escrow will officially close. Some buyers prefer a longer escrow period for various reasons—they need to find another place to live; they're relocating or waiting for school to end—and others want the sale turned around quickly, perhaps for the very same reasons. Regardless, you'll want to make sure you have an escrow officer in mind before you finalize your deal. Your friends, real estate agent, mortgage broker, and loan officer are great resources for helping you find a reputable escrow officer.

TOP SIX REASONS ESCROW FALLS THROUGH

1. Changes in buyer's loan terms
2. Missed deadlines
3. Buyer doesn't have enough cash to close, or there's a delay in getting it
4. Difficulty clearing title
5. Problems paying off existing loan
6. Unresolved contingencies

Now, what exactly does an escrow representative do? The process is not so different from buying a new shirt: Sometimes you need to factor in discounts before you can determine the final cost. In addition, escrow fees usually include state tax and an occasional local charge. In homebuying, an escrow officer figures out the final price you'll pay by itemizing your charges or credits, homeowners' protection insurance, inspection fees, corrective work reimbursements, and other variables. She acts as a mediator of sorts and works on behalf of both the seller and the buyer.

Your escrow officer also ensures that every "t" is crossed and every "i" is dotted in the paperwork, and files it according to law. Her investigation will reveal whether a seller's title is clear for sale, or if your loan comes up short. And if you're not content with contractual obligations in the signed purchase contract (although keep in mind that these requirements must be tangible and clearly stated, not simply things that you interpret as problematic without evidence), you can and should instruct the escrow officer to halt escrow until you are ready.

As you can see, there's a lot of work to be executed in escrow. Kicking back and relaxing aren't options for you (at least not until you've moved your couch into your new home). As Sherry found out, until escrow closes successfully, you're not a homeowner just yet.

Thankfully, your escrow fairy godmother will handle the majority of the annoying ins and outs of the process. But as a smart businesswoman, you'll want to seal your deal as best you can by keeping a close eye on a few escrow details yourself.

First thing to know about escrow: You cannot use your mortgage loan to pay for escrow costs—nor can you charge them to your good ol' credit card. And just so you know, escrow isn't cheap. By asking an escrow officer to prepare an initial statement of your estimated expenses, you can assess approximately how much money you'll need.

If your deal requires you to pay for escrow fees, start going through your files immediately for that $1,000 CD you won back in college for your award-winning poetry. Borrow against your retirement policy. Sell the stock your mom and dad bought to help pay for that yet-to-happen/may-never-happen wedding. No matter where you're getting your liquid money from, do it swiftly and before you need it. Gather a little more than is necessary. You can always return it to savings, or use it to decorate your new home. But the last thing you want is to lose your dream home because you can't front the money by the deadline.

THE 411

Before the fees are due, ask your escrow officer what forms of payment are acceptable. Cashier's check, money order, or bank-wired funds are most often the only acceptable forms of payment.

Now that you know to get your escrow money in order from the outset, what happens next? Your escrow officer will get you a copy of the preliminary title report, a very important document that details for you a number of possible obstacles, as well as restrictions that an association establishes within a community property.

Reviewing your preliminary title report is essential; it's another chance for you to clean up your deal before it becomes final. Concerns like clearing the title for sale—meaning that there are no liens or money owed on a loan or for work performed—are reasonable demands before you close the deal.

If you're purchasing a shared-living space, like a condo or a co-op, here's your chance to thoroughly read the managing board's rules and regulations, which are usually found in the condominium's By-laws and CC&Rs. This task is especially important because many real estate agents or sellers aren't always fully knowledgeable about the building association's rules. So even if you ask them questions during purchase-contract negotiations, they may inadvertently give you inaccurate or misleading information.

Tammy, a newly married, twenty-eight-year-old schoolteacher who purchased a two-bedroom condo as a single woman two years ago faced her own verbal misunderstanding during escrow. Tammy had ended a yearlong relationship with her boyfriend just before buying her new home. She was heartbroken, but her boyfriend wasn't ready to commit and she knew that she owed it to herself to find the inner strength to move on.

Fortunately, Tammy's parents had smartly saved for their daughter's future since she was young. Tammy took charge of her life and used this small fund for a down payment on her first home.

"I was crushed," Tammy said. "I remember feeling lonely amidst my excitement. I had my family's support; I couldn't have done it without them. And buying my place helped me to feel in control. It just seemed surreal that only a year earlier, my life felt so secure and stable, yet it all crumbled overnight. Buying my condo turned out to be the [best] thing I could do for myself, and I needed that comfort during a time like that."

However, Tammy learned the hard way what can happen when you don't carefully read all the policies of a shared-living space. As she was getting over her breakup, she decided she wanted to get a dog, only to find out that her association didn't allow them. Tammy hadn't read over the association's CC&Rs (covenants, conditions, and restrictions) during the escrow process. Tammy's desire to get a dog for companionship and security was dashed.

Over the course of the next year, Tammy and her boyfriend got back together and ultimately got engaged. But these events didn't change her mind about getting a dog. In fact, although she loved her new home and was happy to have her boyfriend back in her life, she came to an unfortunate realization: If she had understood before purchasing her condo that dogs weren't allowed, she probably wouldn't have bought it in the first place. She suffered the consequences of misinformation and not reading the details of the CC&Rs. It was an all-too-common mistake.

A year later, Tammy got her dog after all, but not without a fight. The ever-changing association membership was becoming more evenly divided between longer-term and newer residents, and they were becoming increasingly at odds with one another over numerous issues, especially the right to own dogs.

Through a little investigation and strong-arming, the growing contingency of vocal homeowners who also wanted to be dog owners was finally heard loud and clear. It turned out that the board of directors had been violating homeowners' legal rights regarding this issue for years. California state law had changed, barring homeowners' associations from prohibiting residents of shared-living spaces to own dogs. Subsequently, Leo, a four-month-old cocker spaniel pup, became the newest family member and neighbor in Tammy and Timmy's condominium living quarters.

FIVE COMMON QUESTIONS THAT GET OVERLOOKED

1. Are there any liens against the title?

2. Are pets—dogs, cats, fish—allowed? If so, what are the restrictions (for shared-living spaces)?

3. Do you anticipate increases in any special assessments or homeowners' dues? When was the last time they were raised, and by how much (for shared-living spaces)?

4. Who are your neighbors? Do you have any problems with them?

5. Can you remodel as you like? (Community properties often enforce tight regulations regarding uniformity or plumbing and electrical jobs. Some communities and governments have strict codes pertaining to landscaping, building heights, and other issues.)

Before taking title and sealing the deal in escrow, you need to pay close attention to the final closing statement. By this point, you will have asked your escrow officer how much she expects you'll owe at the end of escrow, but the final closing statement will give you the exact amount by detailing all the financial transactions (debits and credits) and resolved contingencies of the sale.

Before escrow can officially close, you'll need to meet with the escrow representative a couple of days in advance to sign all pertinent documents, like loan papers and the final closing statement. If you haven't already handed over the money, this meeting is when all escrow fees will be due. You'll also need to inform your escrow officer of the name(s) of anyone who will be on the title to your new home.

THE 411

To lock in interest rates, you may face a quick deadline of twenty-four or forty-eight hours to sign your loan documents. Arrange your schedule so that you're available to meet with your escrow officer to sign, seal, and deliver the documents to the lender promptly. Otherwise, you could face increased mortgage rates and delay or entirely uproot escrow.

Taking title is one of the most important decisions you can make for your future. Why? Because it's what a court of law will consider should you need to sell or, dare I say it, face foreclosure.

Buying as a single woman, you'll likely be the sole owner of your property. Tammy took her title on her own because, in a lucky twist, she bought her place in the aftermath of her breakup. Had she and her boyfriend bought together and *then* broken up, they would have found themselves in a highly entangled situation—one that, needless to say, lots of people experience. When two people are on a title, both have decision-making power—and ultimately, after Tammy and her fiancé got married, they decided to add his name to the title as partial owner.

FOUR WAYS TO TAKE TITLE

1. Sole ownership: You, and only you, own your home.

2. Joint tenancy: If you share ownership through joint tenancy (meaning you co-own the property with one or more other people), you, the sole survivor, will automatically become the full owner in case of a partner's death. You also share the responsibility for covering your full mortgage in such a tragedy. This form of ownership also offers a tax-savings opportunity if a partner's death forces you to sell.

3. Community property: This ownership style offers you greater tax savings during the sale of the property than joint tenancy does. This form applies only to married couples. Unlike joint tenancy, community property also allows you to will your share of the home to anyone, or anything, you like—even your beloved cat.

4. Partnerships or tenancies in common: This differs from joint tenancy in that one owner may own a greater share of the co-owned property. No tax savings are offered if you have to sell. However, you do have the legal right to will or sell your share of the property without the other co-owners' consent. Also, ownership of such properties can be divided evenly or unevenly, offering a varied ownership percentage.

If you're blessed to have your family members helping you with your down payment or mortgage, you'll also want to resolve whether their names will go on the title. Weigh the pros and cons: You share profits, but you also share legal and financial responsibilities in a court of law. Your family members' inability to make good on any financial obligations could also reflect poorly on your own credit. For instance, if you expect them to help with the mortgage and they can't fulfill their promise, it's up to you to cover their share; otherwise, you face losing the property.

With the final closing statement signed and the title transferred, you'd better keep your cell phone fully charged and close by. All that's left in the escrow process now is for the escrow officer to record the deed and hand over the money to the seller.

THE 411

A deed is the document that conveys title to real property. A title insurance company must prove that the seller is legally able and free to sell the property to you.

It's important to note that your closing costs and down payment, as well as the mortgage company's payment, must be received by the title insurance company before you can receive the deed. And once that's written in stone . . . yes in-*deed,* you've officially joined the ranks of women homeowners. Congratulations!

sixteen

Ms. Fix-It

n o rent, no deposit. Welcome to your first perks as an official homeowner. With no exorbitant first and last month's
rent to dump (and risk losing) up front, you can relax a bit.
However, there are some nasty little extras you incur when
you're first setting up a new home. Just when you think you've
planned for all that's to come, trust me when I tell you to save
a fund for unexpected expenses. Four other financial areas to
consider when saving to buy your own home include moving expenses, decorating, remodeling, and fixing what wasn't broken
when you bought it.

Moving can be costly. If you want professionals to load,
move, and unload all your belongings for you, expect to pay as
much as $400 or more, depending on how much stuff you own.
If you ask the professionals to pack your things for you, it's quite
a bit more expensive. So if money is an issue—which it very well

could be, since you'll have just forked over a down payment and closing costs out of pocket—consider renting a U-Haul and getting some strong friends to help you move your stuff.

Prior to move-in day, you'll also want to make sure utilities are turned on in your new home. Be prepared to pay a onetime start-up fee or the first month's bill up front. When totaled, it's an expense that could run up to $200 to $300 or more upon move-in. And don't forget about extra luxuries, like a satellite dish, Internet service, TiVo, and so on.

Other expenses that are not necessary, but are worth considering, prior to move-in day include getting a housekeeper to thoroughly clean your home from top to bottom, steam-cleaning your carpeting, and dry-cleaning your drapes or rugs, especially if you negotiated in your contract to inherit them from the seller. These services could cost hundreds of dollars. But if you have the money, complete these tasks before you move in; it'll be a lot easier than it will once you've moved all your furniture in.

Decorating the first home that I owned was an exciting prospect for me. Now that I was a big girl, I wanted to live like one, not like I still lived in an apartment with roommates. I wanted a nice dining room table with matching chairs for entertaining. I wanted a new couch, not the old, slipcovered one my roommate's grandma had gifted us. And I wanted to fill all the cupboard space in my new kitchen with every cooking utensil and wine accessory known to humankind.

Fortunately, I'd reasoned that I wouldn't have a lot of money to decorate with once I depleted my savings for a down payment and closing costs. Purchasing a nice leather chair here, a coffee table there, and a complete matching bedroom set while I rented felt like a way to invest in my home even before I owned it. As it turned out, my long-term planning for adulthood paid off nicely. While I was actively negotiating to buy my home, I envisioned exactly where my armoire might go, picked the perfect spot for my leather chair, and measured the master bedroom's square footage to ensure that my big princess bed and dresser would fit perfectly. But when I moved in, despite my years of preplanning and purchasing quality pieces of furniture, I quickly realized I would need to buy even more to fill the empty spaces in my new home. Depending on your tastes, accomplishing that goal can cost hundreds to thousands of dollars.

Unless you specifically purchased your home as a fixer-upper, make sure to fully weigh the pros and cons of any remodeling before making the investment. Consider factors like how long you expect to live in your home, whether you'll be nearly draining your savings if you choose to do serious remodeling, and how much those projects will increase the value of your property. Also decide whether you have the time and resources to coordinate and oversee the work.

You also need to keep in mind what types of renovations are important to you. Basic renovations include things like installing a washer and dryer, hardwood floors, or central air; landscaping; remodeling the kitchen; adding an extra bathroom; or putting in more closet space. All of these alterations can be very expensive. However, they can also be solid investments that will increase your property's value—not to mention make your living space much more enjoyable.

You can easily make plenty of other, less expensive cosmetic changes in your home that will both personalize it and make it appear more valuable, including painting the interior; adding decorative touches, like crown molding, fancy light switch plates, and chandeliers; or installing more functional additives, like a ceiling fan or air conditioner.

THE 411

Capital improvement is money you spend to permanently increase your property's value and life, on such enhancements as new appliances, roofing, heating, landscaping, or a new kitchen. The difference between what you originally paid for your home and the amount you sell it for is known as your capital gain. Bottom line: Save all your receipts for any such home renovations you pay for. The IRS allows you to add the value of capital improvements to the price you paid to buy your home, ultimately minimizing the amount of money you'll owe in taxes upon selling (this process is called adjusted cost basis).

Keep in mind that if you buy a co-op, town home, or condominium, you're often required to get your homeowners' board of directors' approval for renovations, even in your private unit. Anything that affects the home's structural foundation, or community plumbing and electricity, cannot be changed without your first getting the board's permission. And even seemingly minor upgrades that can be seen from outside your unit, like sliding glass doors, window frames, doors, and balcony and railing decor, are all subject to approval.

THE 411

Alterations that get your home up to par—to meet codes or fix problems with plumbing, electricity, and other structural issues— are repairs, not renovations. These repairs often cost beaucoup bucks but, because they're repairs and not improvements, add little increased value to your home in resale. Repairs are also not tax deductible.

Shared-living properties also involve shared, and often conflicting, opinions about how to keep up and improve the property's common areas. Does the building need painting, and do the majority of the homeowners agree? If so, what color paint should be used, and how much money does the community think is a fair amount to spend? Do you want a Jacuzzi installed in the back-patio community area? The majority of your complex's homeowners need to agree as well. Do you want to upgrade the foyer? Better hope your neighbors want to spend money from the reserves to do that. You get the picture.

In a freestanding single-family home, you'll have more say in the remodeling process. However, you may find yourself coming head to head with neighbors or nearby businesses who are bothered by your renovations, or who are involved in their own renovating or landscaping projects and thereby impact you. You might find that the roots in your neighbor's oak tree cause you plumbing issues, for instance. Or maybe your neighbors are considering adding another story to their home that would block your mountain view. Perhaps you live in an industrial neighborhood where a local business has plans to build a parking structure virtually in your backyard, obstructing your views and creating congestion.

THE 411

Many home renovations require city permits before work can begin. Failure to acquire a permit can result in hefty fines and even poor workmanship. With city permits, city-approved inspectors examine the work, making sure it's to code. For some of us gals who aren't so skilled in DIY work, this permit can be especially beneficial. Ask your contractor, engineer, or architect if your renovation job requires a city permit, or contact your local government housing agency directly.

Getting involved in your community and knowing your neighbors are great ways to ward off issues before they become problems. Befriend your elderly next-door neighbor. Attend local government meetings when you can, and get informed. Serve on the board of your governing association, or attend its monthly meetings and voice your opinion. The more people you know who have the power to influence the quality of your living space, the more likely they'll want to keep you content and keep you as a neighbor.

THE 411

Your neighbors and community leaders can also serve as great resources for referrals to professional maintenance help.

After all the time I'd devoted to finding a home, qualifying for a loan, negotiating my offer, and pulling through escrow, I didn't think about any maintenance issues I might face upon moving in. After all, I had opted to buy a home that didn't need any work because I didn't want to have to worry about those kinds of problems.

But I learned my first lesson as a homeowner when, just two weeks after I moved in, my garbage disposal broke and the sliding glass doors to my shower derailed. I realized quickly that there's no such thing as hassle-free homeowning. If you don't want to have to pay for most home repairs yourself, rent.

My new electric self-cleaning oven was way more intimidating than my childhood plug-in Betty Crocker oven had been. It had a lot more buttons and functions, and it wasn't childproofed, or Jennifer-proofed, for that matter. I was ecstatic to finally have a dishwasher . . . until the rollers went off track. My refrigerator worked swell and was practically brand-new, so when the ice-maker started gushing water, I was bewildered. With two toilets and two showers, I had double trouble on my hands. And with two balconies, I had twice as many sliding glass doors and screens to contend with. As a new homeowner, you should expect the un-expected. If it ain't broke, anticipate that it will be. Get ahead of the game! Form your A and B maintenance teams of people who can help you when unforeseeable disasters strike.

NOT A DIY GIRL?

Newer homes may come with amenities that carry warranties. Some sellers may have purchased insurance on their appliances that extends under your ownership. If not, consider buying ap-pliance insurance, which works like this: Your insurer will send a professional to your home to diagnose, and possibly repair, the problem for a nominal fee to you (like $50). But, as with any insurance, your problem may or may not be covered, depending on what kind of coverage you have and what the problem is. To investigate further, go online and check out appliance insurance and your location. Or inquire with a few local appliance stores to see if they work with any insurance companies.

Which and how many specialists you'll need to help you maintain your home depends on the kind of home you've purchased and all the amenities that came with it. First things first: Start a home-maintenance reference list. For starters, you'll need a plumber, electrician, pest-control expert, and overall handyperson. You may also need a landscaper, painter, locksmith, roofer, pool technician, housekeeper, contractor, or any combination thereof.

Without a landlord to address your problems, you'll make your life a whole lot easier as a new homeowner if you have helpful, trustworthy people taking care of daily living issues, like overflowing toilets or leaky faucets. You should learn to fix the simple things yourself, of course, but sometimes even the most basic task, like hanging heavy shelving or fixing a door or window that's stuck or off track, can seem overwhelming in your already full life. An extra pair (or pairs) of hands can be invaluable. Consider developing a list of A and B maintenance teams for competitive pricing, and for emergencies when your preferred plumber or electrician isn't around to help when you're in a pinch.

Shop around for good help. Remember, you want to get people who come with solid referrals. If you don't know anyone who's previously used the person you're going to hire, make sure to request references from that person, and actually call them. You can also contact your local Better Business Bureau to make sure no bad reports have been filed against the person you want to hire, or the company they work for. Also make sure to ask for proof that they are licensed, bonded, and insured. Request their state-issued license number, and look up their license at your local city hall and Better Business Bureau.

SAFETY FIRST

Whenever possible—and especially for your personal safety—it's best to hire professionals whom others you trust have used. As a single woman, you're putting yourself in a vulnerable position simply by allowing a stranger into your home. Before you have someone over, check references. If you speak with a professional on the phone who creeps you out, listen to your instincts and don't hire them. If possible, invite a friend over when you meet the professional the first couple of times.

Hiring help is essential for accomplished working women like us. We have a tendency to overextend ourselves in other areas of our lives, like our jobs or our families, and we often put ourselves second or third on our list of people to take care of. And although home professionals can be expensive, take time to judge the things you think you can do against the things you can actually do. It's not worth the damage you might cause trying to fix something just because you don't want to spend the extra money. Clearly, the decision to hire help or do it yourself will vary from woman to woman, and there will be plenty of home-maintenance tasks you can tackle all by your lonesome. You'll be amazed by how empowered you feel once you've succeeded in fixing the garbage disposal or that overflowing toilet on your own. It'll also help you save money, especially if you end up hiring someone who tries to overcharge you. Plus, some emergencies can't wait a day for someone to respond. Learn how to fix that overflowing toilet on your own. And if you simply can't get around hiring a professional, don't forget to call a number of candidates and get competitive bids.

seventeen

Buyer's Remorse

F unny, isn't it? We never heard what happened to Cinderella after she and the prince ran off and got married. Sure, I know—they lived happily ever after. But do you think Cinderella ever dealt with moments of doubt when she and the prince fought? Of course her life as a princess was a lot better than living with her wicked stepmom and stepsisters. But don't you suppose Cinderella wanted to kick the prince to the curb on occasion?

Now that you're a homeowner, know that it's okay if, upon moving in, you're slapped in the face by some hardcore realities. Maybe you expected happily ever after with your new home. Perhaps you were caught up in the fairy tale of smooth sailing after all the paperwork was finished. It happens to the best of us. So don't think you're alone if you feel buyer's remorse when your first mortgage bill comes, or if you start questioning your decision to buy as soon as water floods your home after a major rainstorm or your refrigerator breaks down. You may feel buyer's remorse repeatedly—like every time property taxes are due—or it may take a while for the regret to kick in. Perhaps you won't feel it until one day when you're forced to decline joining a girlfriends' getaway because you don't have the money for your mortgage and the trip.

Buying a home can send single women into a tailspin. It's empowering and fun, but it can also often be depressing, limiting our access to the things we love and making us feel like we have a big burden to carry all alone, and nowhere to turn for support. If you feel the rush of homeowning starting to overwhelm you and you start second-guessing your decision, it's time to revisit some of the reasons why you chose to buy in the first place:

1. You bought because you were making a long-term investment for yourself—and in yourself.

2. You bought because you were ready to make your home your own, and to live the way you wanted, with little say from anyone else.

3. You bought because you needed a tax write-off.

4. You bought because you could.

And just when you thought your regret was a passing feeling, you'll be barraged with offers in the mail from loan and insurance companies soliciting your business. If no one told you to expect this onslaught, you just might entertain some of these offers. But I'm here to warn you: Don't go there. Ignore them. Most of these solicitations don't provide you with beneficial coverage—and they're overpriced. Plus, you may already be sufficiently covered in other areas (like loss of pay due to illness) through your company's paid disability insurance.

FOUR TYPES OF SOLICITATIONS TO EXPECT AS A NEW HOMEOWNER

1. Mortgage lenders: Now that the loan companies know you're a viable candidate, they'll be clamoring to seduce you with offers to transfer your loan over to them. Keep in mind any penalties you'll face if you switch loans too early. Also, talk to your accountant or mortgage broker before taking the plunge. Most solicitations are written to entice you, but are no better than the loan you already have.

2. Mortgage insurance companies: For a fee, these companies offer protection to you in case you can't make a mortgage payment. Typically, however, the amount of protection they offer doesn't meet the amount you need, and this type of insurance can be expensive. You can consider supplementing it with long-term disability insurance if you're worried.

3. Homestead offers: Homesteading means protecting your home's equity from lawsuits. Much of the service these companies offer you for an inflated fee is work you can do on your own through your local government agencies. If you're in a situation where you deem it necessary to protect your home against potential lawsuits, file the appropriate papers through your local recorder's office.

4. Long-term debt-reducing offers: These companies offer a service you can do yourself, and they charge you a monthly fee for it. And perhaps you've selected the longer-term payoff for good reason, such as wanting more money to stash in your high interest–earning "in case I lose my job" fund, your house-maintenance nest egg, or your 401(k) retirement account.

My thirty-six-year-old friend Rianna saved just over $50,000 over the course of seven years, and that money became her security blanket. She'd always intended to spend it on a down payment for a home someday, but once she'd managed to save such a large chunk of change, she became fearful of letting it go.

"Here I am, nearing my forties and single," she tells me. "I've been dating a guy for six months, and although I love him, neither of us knows where it's going for certain. I've been in my same job for a decade, and while my company treats me well, I'm so over it. I'm bored. I want to do something different; I'm just not sure what. So when it came to buying a home, I was skeptical. I already didn't want to be in my job, and a hefty mortgage would not only handcuff me to it, but I also wouldn't have my nest egg to fall back on in case I couldn't take it anymore or I was laid off. I was torn."

After looking for a condo halfheartedly for a couple of years, Rianna finally decided to finally take the search more seriously. Eventually she fell for one, and recently entered escrow. "I am completely freaked out by it," she confesses. "Now I only have one paycheck's worth of savings to support me if something happens. But buying this place at this time just felt like it was the right thing to do."

I can understand Rianna's fear. With no secondary income to alleviate any potential hardship, her primary safety net is now frayed, so all she has to rely on is herself. Rianna just needs to make sure she pays her mortgage on time each month and shifts her focus to saving, saving, saving.

THE 411

Financial experts suggest that people keep a minimum of three to six months' worth of living expenses in an account that can become liquid at any moment.

With much of your money tied up in your home investment, it's time to get cracking on building up your emergency cash reserves. There's a strong possibility that you won't be able to save as much each month, because your mortgage will likely be higher, or at least equal, to your rent. That's understandable, but you can review your budget and decide on a figure you think you could comfortably live without each week—say, $75—and have your financial advisor deduct it automatically from your paycheck and deposit it into your money market or savings account. In four short weeks, you'll have saved $300. In one year, that's $3,600, and in three years you'll have saved nearly $11,000. And if you put the money in a high interest–earning money market mutual fund, your total will likely increase even faster.

Saving is half the battle. Take it from me: It's not how much you make, but how much you spend that counts. I'm the last person to tell you not to enjoy the finer things in life; I certainly don't advocate giving up pampering yourself, traveling, or other luxuries that make you feel great. You work hard for your money, so to not take pleasure in life . . . well, that would be a sin. However,

I do recommend prioritizing and minimizing how much, and how often, you engage in unnecessary spending. Determine needs versus wants: You need to eat daily, but do you need to pay someone for a weekly manicure? If an extra indulgence like this encroaches too much on rebuilding your emergency-reserves fund, it's time to take a break from paying for it.

Sometimes saving money costs money. Making your home more energy efficient by doing things like adding solar panels or insulation, landscaping for more shade, or installing devices that better manage household water flow can make for year-round savings. You can also check into utility management programs through services like your electrical company. And while we're on the topic of utilities, you can cut costs and help the environment by being mindful of energy-sucking habits like leaving the lights on when you don't need to, or running heating and cooling systems when no one is home.

Another way to cover your monthly mortgage payment and save money is to find additional income. How, you ask? If you bought a home with two or more bedrooms, ask yourself if you really need all that space for just one person. Perhaps you could take on a tenant. As the official landlord, you're ultimately in charge of how the house is run and how much a renter will pay for her room—but keep in mind that you're also responsible for fixing things in a timely fashion if they break. And you have to be willing to look the other way if your tenant doesn't treat your property exactly as you would. Taking on a renter won't be an ideal situation for some, but it's good to weigh all your options. Ask your tax accountant what makes sense in the grand scheme of your finances. If you do take on a roommate, do so on a trial basis by limiting her tenancy to a year lease. You will likely find that she's a positive addition, as her rent payment will enable you to build up your emergency fund relatively quickly and easily.

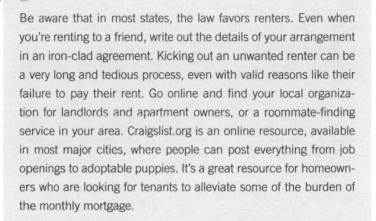

THE 411

Be aware that in most states, the law favors renters. Even when you're renting to a friend, write out the details of your arrangement in an iron-clad agreement. Kicking out an unwanted renter can be a very long and tedious process, even with valid reasons like their failure to pay their rent. Go online and find your local organization for landlords and apartment owners, or a roommate-finding service in your area. Craigslist.org is an online resource, available in most major cities, where people can post everything from job openings to adoptable puppies. It's a great resource for homeowners who are looking for tenants to alleviate some of the burden of the monthly mortgage.

To live monthly, not month to month, without feeling like you're living just to pay your mortgage or to help build your emergency fund, you may want to review your current paycheck deductions for your retirement. Depending on your financial goals, you might decide that it's helpful to decrease the percentage you have withdrawn until you become comfortable with your monthly budget. Certainly, you'll want to maximize your earning opportunities if your company matches part of the amount you invest in your future each month. But if you want to build up cash reserves you may need in the next couple of years, perhaps investing less in your 401(k) for the time being isn't quite so terrible. Consult your financial advisor about what will help you best achieve your goals.

At the end of the day, you'll find a way. You've done your homework and bought within your means. Tying up a few loose ends will simply alleviate added stress. Most important, remember that you did the right thing.

eighteen

Relocating, Refinancing, and Renewing Your Vows

L ife is fluid. Sure, we can try to control it and keep it the same in our attempts to feel safe during uncertain times. We can plan our futures and attempt to steer life down the path we choose. But if the universe calls on you for change and growth, be assured that you'll be a casualty of its desires. I use the word "casualty" because sometimes forces beyond your control come on like an emotional storm and toss you around until you feel torn and broken down. Other times, the cosmos reveals its wishes more gently and lovingly. Either way, you're forever affected by the experiences life has conspired to offer you. How you roll with the punches, well, that's up to you.

"I had just started dating my boyfriend shortly after going into escrow on my new home," says twenty-seven-year-old magazine marketing executive Christina. "About four months into our relationship, we agreed he'd move in. I was elated! The quarters would be tight in my quaint one-bedroom pad, but we didn't care. We were in love. And financially, it was a good move for us both—a way for us to start a fund for our dream of taking a year off for traveling abroad."

Six months later, Christina and her boyfriend broke up. "It was tough for a while," she says. "We still had to live together for a couple months while he looked for a suitable place to rent."

Christina decided that continuing to live in the place where she and her boyfriend had been in love and then gone through such hard times would be too much for her. "I needed an escape," she admits. "I had always wanted to live in New York, and now was the perfect time . . . except now I had my home to contend with. What was I going to do? Sell? Rent it out? Stay? Ugh! *What have I tied myself into?* I remember thinking. I felt stuck."

Christina ultimately concluded that a change of scenery was just what she needed, and she decided that she wanted to move to New York after all. She took it on as an adventure, and knew that somehow she'd make it happen. She put her home up for rent once she landed a job in New York. She wasn't sure, after all, that relocating was going to work out for her in the long run, so she committed to it for one year and knew she could return to her house in California whenever she was ready to. Christina is a great example of the options you have as a homeowner: She may have decided to rent her place out, but she certainly could have sold it, too. Single women's lives often change rapidly, depending on our jobs, relationships, and new opportunities. It's important to realize that committing to buying a new home doesn't necessarily lock you into your current situation or lifestyle, which could very well change in the next few years.

Though Christina was concerned about paying her monthly mortgage and association fees with the rent she'd be getting from her tenant, she reasoned that as long as the price difference was nominal, it would be worth it for her. "If I rented in New York and shared the cost with a roommate, I could swing both my monthly rent and the additional few hundred dollars of my monthly mortgage payment. Then I'd just have to come up with the property taxes every six months," Christina concludes.

Everything fell into place when Christina landed the gig of her dreams, working for a popular lifestyle magazine for women, a few months into her job search. "I couldn't believe it!" Christina says. "It didn't feel real, because I'd wanted this moment for so long. And this job was so much better than the other opportunities that had passed me by."

Within four weeks, Christina was busy situating her things in her new apartment in the Big Apple. But by the time she moved to New York, she still hadn't rented out her condo back in Los Angeles. She'd had plenty of applicants, but her home was an investment in her future, and finding just the right tenant to take pride in and care for it was important to her.

Christina turned to a reputable Los Angeles property-management company for help, and made peace with the fact that for at least a month or two, she'd need to cover both her New York rent and her mortgage payment. It was a sacrifice worth making to ensure that the right people moved in. "Yeah, the double monthly rent was going to strap me. I had to pull a little padding out of my savings to back me," Christina says. "But with the law in favor of renters, I didn't want to end up in a battle, trying to evict my tenant."

GOOD HELP IS HARD TO FIND

If you elect to move and will be renting out your property, consider hiring a property-management company. For a monthly fee, the company will find suitable renters and will be responsible for addressing day-to-day maintenance issues that pop up. The company will also handle monthly financial and legal transactions. Be sure to search for a well-respected and insured company with offices in the area where your property is. Ask friends and family members for references, investigate online, or look in your local phone book for property-management companies in your city. You can also ask your realtor for recommendations. Finally, consider employing a friend or family member you trust to be your property manager. Just make sure to solicit the help of an attorney to write up your leasing contract.

Sure enough, just a month after Christina's move east, her property manager found a young, professional married couple who loved her home and wanted to move in. Their financial history checked out, and their former landlords and references had nothing but positive things to say. They signed a year lease and all was set. And Christina could breathe comfortably knowing her property-management company was also handling any maintenance issues that arose. "It was a relief," Christina confesses. "I could just dive into kicking butt at my new job and focus on creating a social network."

A move across the country or abroad may not be in your cards. Instead of a big life change, perhaps your opportunity to grow will transpire right in your own backyard. You may have purchased your place as a three- to five-year investment. You might hope that by then you'll have found yourself a home that you want to live in for many years, or that you'll have found a partner to share it with. But what if the universe has other plans for you, and staying put is your immediate calling? Refinancing just may be your next step. Refinancing is when you take out a new loan mortgage to replace your old.

THE 411

If you want to refinance because of a lower-interest-rate market, you might be able to bypass any prepayment penalty charge by giving your current lender the opportunity to create the new mortgage. Make your first call to your current loan institution to see if they can give you a good deal.

Hopefully you secured a great interest rate on your mortgage loan when you bought your home. Interest rates, however, are in constant flux, so whether your fixed-loan term is about to expire or current interest rates dip well below what you cemented at the

time of purchase, keep an eye on what's happening in the market.
It could help you save some of your hard-earned cash.

THE 411

The less interest you pay on your mortgage, the less you can
deduct from and write off on your annual taxes.

ESSENTIAL QUESTIONS ABOUT REFINANCING

1. Do you have a loan (pre-refinancing) that will charge
   you a penalty if you pay it off before the end of a specific
   time period?

2. How will a new mortgage loan affect your tax situation?

3. With the new loan (post-refinancing), how long will you be
   tied to your home, and will you face any new penalties for
   selling your home or paying off the loan before a specified
   time frame ends?

4. How long do you plan on living in your home?

5. How will refinancing affect your credit?

6. What is the total cost of refinancing—including things like
   title insurance and loan fees—going to be?

You may be hesitant to refinance. After all, the up-front costs
may not save you money on the back end. On the other hand,
refinancing just may be the answer to your prayers. Outline with

a mortgage lender, banker, or broker all of the details that refinancing involves.

The important thing to remember as a new homeowner is that you're rarely stuck. The beauty of the situation is that you have a place to call your own, and you have an investment that will help you get going if you decide you want out.

Christina, for example, took advantage of her position as a homeowner. She was able to follow her dreams of moving east while keeping her safety net intact. Doing so made going back to L.A. a viable option, and she was ready to do just that after a two-year stint in New York City. She thoroughly enjoyed her stay in New York, her career flourished, and she had her home in Santa Monica waiting for her. It just goes to show you: You never know where life is going to take you.

resources

BOOKS

Bach, David, *Smart Women Finish Rich: 9 Steps to Achieving Financial Security and Funding Your Dreams*. Broadway Books, 2002.

Brown, Ray, and Eric Tyson, MBA, *Home Buying for Dummies, Third Edition*. Wiley Publishing, 2006.

Degregori, Patty, and Jennifer Musselman, *The Hip Girl's Handbook for Home, Car & Money Stuff*. Wildcat Canyon Press, 2002.

Fletcher, Patty, and Jennifer Musselman, *The Hip Girl's Handbook for the Working World*. Wildcat Canyon Press, 2005.

Hymer, Dian, *House Hunting: The Take-Along Workbook for Home Buyers*. Chronicle Books, 2002.

Orman, Suze, *The 9 Steps to Financial Freedom: Practical and Spiritual Steps So You Can Stop Worrying*. Three Rivers Press, 2006.

Summers, Vanessa, *Buying Solo: The Single Woman's Guide to Buying a First Home*. Perigee Books/Penguin Group, 2005.

ONLINE CREDIT RESOURCES

www.equifax.com

www.experian.com

www.tuc.com

 ## MAGAZINES

Each of these magazines features homes and rooms that can help you visualize your dream house.

Architectural Digest

Better Homes and Gardens

Domino

Midwest Living

O, the Oprah Magazine

 ## LOAN WEBSITES AND ONLINE MORTGAGE RESOURCES

www.bankofamerica.com; www.prudential.com
Reputable and long-standing financial institutions, lenders, and insurance companies that can help you gauge what's available to you are important. Shop around and don't just rely on one company.

www.eloan.com
A well-known, mortgage-specific website with lists of loans from numerous lenders. The site offers loan consultants through a toll-free number and allows you to track pending loan offers.

www.fanniemae.com; www.freddiemac.com; www.homepath.com
These websites offer loans to potential homebuyers, as well as some explanations of basic mortgage and homebuying jargon and processes. They're ideal sites for credit-challenged candidates to visit, or for those who qualify for low- or no-money-down programs, which are also particularly beneficial for first-time homebuyers.

www.hsh.com
The site offers up-to-date information about topics including fluctuating interest rates and loan options, as well as resources and articles about homebuying and mortgages.

www.hud.gov
The U.S. Department of Housing Under Development is a government-assistance agency. It helps secure loans for qualifying candidates looking to buy homes by insuring lenders against potential loss.

GEOGRAPHICAL SAFETY WEBSITES

www.meganslaw.com
Read up on registered sex offenders in the area surrounding your potential new home.

www.ncpc.org
Provides tips and suggestions for disaster preparedness.

about the author

© Rena Durham

ᴊennifer Musselman is the coauthor of *The Hip Girl's Handbook for the Working World* and coauthor of *The Hip Girl's Handbook for Home, Car & Money Stuff*. Musselman has also been published in *Shape, Seventeen, Teen, CosmoGirl,* and *Twist* magazines. She purchased her first home, in Santa Monica, California, in 2006, where she recently served as president of her homeowners' association. Since Musselman bought her home, her second suit has become an apron—she enjoys hosting dinner parties with friends and experimenting in the kitchen. She shares her home with Leo, her playful and loving puppy, who runs the house.